Teaching History

Praise for *Teaching History*

The history curriculum is a battleground that tells us more about who we are in the present than who we were in the past. Sorting through the hue and cry to discern legitimate differences can be a challenge. In this new book, Jonathon Dallimore offers an indispensable roadmap for navigating a field too often driven by partisanship and emotion instead of reasoned argument. This volume will be invaluable for young teachers just starting out. But it will be equally beneficial for veterans seeking to be reinvigorated by a fresh overview of the curricular landscape. It merits a place on every history teacher's bookshelf.

Professor Sam Wineburg (Margaret Jacks Professor of Education Emeritus, Stanford University)

Practical, authoritative and engaging are the words that instantly spring to mind reading this book! Dallimore has written a generous and insightful guide to the challenges and opportunities of history teaching.

Professor Anna Clark (University of Technology, Sydney)

As an active head teacher working with early career history teachers, this book is incredibly helpful. Dallimore has provided a blend of current research with realistic quandaries to give both new teachers and their mentors the opportunity to engage in meaningful conversations. More importantly, this book is a reminder for all history teachers about why we chose this profession. An engaging, enjoyable and thought-provoking read from an author who genuinely understands the joy of teaching history.

Martin Douglas (Secondary Head of History)

This book is a must-have for anyone starting on their history teaching journey. In the book, Jonathon provides a clear framework for teaching history and a wide range of helpful suggestions for how to put it into practice. As I was reading, I made note of many useful ideas that I'm eager to implement in the classroom.

Kate White (early career history teacher)

Jonathon Dallimore has presented a wonderful introduction to teaching secondary history for beginning teachers. This rich and engaging read is filled with relatable anecdotes and experiences directly from the classroom and life as an educator. With practical strategies and genuine advice, Dallimore has created a fantastic guide to being a successful history teacher for those just starting their journey in this role.

Marisa Thamsirisup (recent graduate)

Teaching History

A Practical Guide for Secondary School Teachers

JONATHON DALLIMORE

No generative artificial intelligence was used in the writing of this book.

Published in 2025 by Amba Press, Melbourne, Australia
www.ambapress.com.au

© Jonathon Dallimore 2025

All rights reserved. No part of this book may be reproduced or transmitted in any form or by any means, electronic or mechanical, including photocopying, recording or by any information storage and retrieval system, without prior permission in writing from the publisher.

Cover design: Tess McCabe
Internal design: Amba Press
Editor: Andrew Campbell

ISBN: 9781923215481 (pbk)
ISBN: 9781923215498 (ebk)

A catalogue record for this book is available from the National Library of Australia.

Contents

Acknowledgments		ix
Prologue		xi
Introduction		1

Part One: Setting Foundations — 9

Chapter 1	Take joy in the subject	11
Chapter 2	Value and nurture your subject expertise	16
Chapter 3	Develop a vision for why you teach history	24
Chapter 4	Treat history as a holistic process	32
Chapter 5	Adapt the discipline for schools	42
Chapter 6	Nurture your curriculum confidence	56
Chapter 7	Learn to use curriculum documents	64
Chapter 8	Aim to engage, not entertain	68

Part Two: Planning – Year Levels and Topics — 77

Chapter 9	Balance clarity, direction and flexibility	79
Chapter 10	Use, adapt or plan thoughtful topic sequences	84
Chapter 11	Do not treat all content as equal	90
Chapter 12	Break each topic into manageable parts	93
Chapter 13	Work towards smaller and larger cumulative goals	97
Chapter 14	Use inquiry questions to guide the whole and the parts	102
Chapter 15	Keep major assessments embedded and coherent	107

Part Three: Sequences and Lessons — 115

Chapter 16	Work on developing content, complexity and communication	117
Chapter 17	Aim to challenge and support every student	123
Chapter 18	Anticipate errors and misconceptions	130
Chapter 19	Use historical sources meaningfully	136
Chapter 20	Engage with historical interpretations meaningfully	147
Chapter 21	Use particular pedagogies to solve subject problems	157
Chapter 22	Consider weight, energy and mode in your lessons	167
Chapter 23	Revisit, consolidate and connect learning regularly	177
Chapter 24	Make stories and analogies a natural part of your teaching	188
Chapter 25	Save time with some templates that you can adapt	195
Chapter 26	Make intentional use of feedback	202

Epilogue — 208

Acknowledgments

It is difficult to know where to begin and end acknowledgments for a book such as this. It draws on a significant amount of personal experience as a student and a teacher and also on specific input from individuals who have read and commented on early drafts of the work. Perhaps it makes sense to proceed in a rough chronological manner.

First, my family. I was fortunate to grow up surrounded by ideas and books and conversation. My parents were, and are, open-minded and never judgmental about the ideas my brothers and I wanted to discuss or explore. Nothing was off the table, and I distinctly remember beginning to appreciate that as a teenager as we read and discussed the lyrics in good music, read and argued about religion and philosophy and welcomed many different people into our orbit. I am convinced that this, and being forced by our grandfather Jack to watch *The Lighthorsemen* as young boys, contributed profoundly to my love of history and, ultimately, to the ideas in this book.

Then, to my own history teachers. Although I was not always the most able student or the easiest to teach, I doubt that I would be as deeply immersed in the world of history and history education as I am now if I did not have a positive experience of history in my own schooling. Particularly in my senior years, I came to love history even though it was easier to get good marks in music and mathematics. It is hard to pin down, but I think the way the subject was presented as something enjoyable, productive and useful made it stand out among the subjects I completed.

At university, I was fortunate too to have learned from so many interesting and diverse historians and scholars. Despite all the jokes and the way such degrees are now maligned in discourse and government policy, my undergraduate arts degree was a wonderful and well-rounded education covering history, literature, philosophy, geography and sociology. Combined with what I learned from my history teachers in secondary school, I can see how many of the ideas in this book have been shaped by those formative experiences too.

As a teacher at both schools and universities, my ideas have also been profoundly shaped by the students I have been fortunate to teach and by many colleagues. I remember being in awe of those teachers whom I worked with in my early years as a new teacher: the way they could work productively with difficult classes, make sense of confusing curriculum documents, bring history to life in simple and complex ways, and not take themselves too seriously in the process.

The network of history teachers connected to the History Teachers' Association of New South Wales has also been a great inspiration over many years for me. I distinctly remember going to my first large HTANSW event in the early 2000s and thinking: "Imagine doing that?!" It has been a genuine privilege to be involved in that community in a more direct way over the last 10 years as both a volunteer and now an employee.

More specifically, many people also contributed directly to the crafting of this book. Michael Spurr helped shape the basic idea in conversations about what it might look like. Anna Clark, Lindsay Gibson, Kate Cameron, Denis Mootz, Linda Kovacs, Penny Van Bergen, Martin Douglas, Marisa Thamsirisup, Natasha Mercer, Thomas Powell, Kate White, Vivienne Bui and Ken Webb all read early drafts, and their comments and questions vastly improved the result, at times saving me from the embarrassment of presenting poorly formed ideas to the wider public. Clearly any problems that remain rest on my shoulders only.

Thanks also to Alicia Cohen and the team at Amba Press for giving this book a chance. The process from start to finish has been one based on trust, professionalism and support. As an author, I could not have asked for more and I do appreciate the work that goes into projects such as this.

Lastly, to Jean and Otis. This book took me away some evenings and weekends and it left me more tired than usual at other times. Finishing a big project like this also brings a deep satisfaction that is hard to explain, so thank you for your patience and support. Otis, whatever you decide to do in life, I hope that seeing your dad tackle work like this helps you keep your eyes wide. It is just a ride after all.

Prologue

After completing a one-year Graduate Diploma in Education, I began my teaching career doing a mix of casual relief days and some shorter blocks of teaching across a range of different government schools in New South Wales. The school I worked in mostly once I graduated was one in which I had completed a six-week practicum, and it had a high level of behavioural challenges. I quickly learned that the experience as a day-to-day casual teacher could vary widely depending on which faculty I was in on the day – some head teachers provided a lot of support; others basically left you to fend for yourself. I found it a steep and, at times, difficult learning curve but one that helped me develop useful instincts when it came to managing student behaviour and developing a sense of professional presence within a classroom.

Following work in other similar schools, I later managed to get more consistent and then permanent work at a very different school where there were fewer significant behavioural problems. At that school, most lessons could focus on teaching and learning without sustained disruption. Most students would complete the tasks they were given in class and submit major assessments on time. At this school I was able to spend much more time creating new resources and experimenting with different ways to teach.

I remember my first few years of teaching as a tornado of experience, and I am certain that I made many mistakes. I am genuinely grateful for the variety of the experiences, but I also enjoyed getting the opportunity to establish roots in different places at different times. For the most part, I enjoyed the opportunity to know these school communities (the students, the families and the teachers) closely over more extended periods.

Over the past several years I have had the opportunity to think back over these earlier stages of my career more reflectively. I now realise very clearly that across these varied contexts I was learning to manage myself as a teacher mainly through a combination of the advice I had been given, following the guidance of the more effective teachers I worked with, and trial and error (is there any other way?). I was learning how to introduce a new topic to a new class, how to interact with a student exhibiting aggressive behaviour, how to support a demoralised student, how to explain an assessment task, the food to avoid if I wanted to escape a dreaded mid-afternoon slump in energy, and when to go to the printing room to avoid a long wait for the photocopier.

As important as all this was, I was also learning how to teach my subject, history. I had been fortunate to have brilliant history teachers in senior school (Mrs Stasiukynas and Mrs O'Shea), mostly excellent teachers at university, outstanding teachers in my subject-specific courses during my teaching degree and, with one or two exceptions, wonderful mentors and colleagues in the schools I worked in. But for all the expert modelling I could draw on, I had to make the job my own. I now had to pose the questions, set the activities, explain (and re-explain) the new concepts, set and manage the assessment tasks, and provide the feedback on student work.

This is the aspect of teaching (and education more generally) that has inspired me more than any other. I love history and when I decided to become a teacher, I wanted to be a history teacher. I love thinking and talking about history and I enjoy discussing how to teach it. Since 2015 I have been fortunate to be able to work extensively with history teachers across New South Wales, Australia and internationally to design and deliver professional learning for history teachers at varying stages of their careers. Since 2016 I have also had the privilege of teaching annual classes to pre-service history teachers at the University of New South Wales (Sydney) and the University of Wollongong, introducing them to the profession.

This book was born out of those two dimensions of my unfolding career: learning to teach history myself and teaching those entering the profession. It collates tips that I was given and adapted and others that I figured out more independently (but certainly not in isolation). It is not an attempt to provide a complete or authoritative handbook for teaching history. It is offered as a brief introduction to a limited set of ideas and to complement the wide variety of books, articles, blogs and podcasts now available that explore broader issues in teaching and history education.

This is a book that I believe I would have benefited greatly from as I set out on this path 20 years ago. It is primarily designed for early-career history teachers broadly defined as those studying to become history teachers and those in the first five years of their teaching career. It may also benefit more established teachers of other subjects with little to no background in history or history education taking classes in this area for the first time. It may even help veteran teachers looking for some fresh ideas or ways of communicating the challenges of teaching history to younger colleagues. Above all, I hope this book helps to make some people's entry into the world of history teaching a little easier and more enjoyable.

Introduction

The teaching profession demands a lot from those who decide to join its ranks. In secondary schools, teachers' attention is bombarded from many angles, most days of the week. There is the teaching angle (being in a class with students teaching), the welfare angle, the social angle, the collegial angle, the professional angle, and so on. No wonder that on some days it can take considerable time to decompress once the final bell rings.

Then there is the scholarly and public commentary: the seemingly endless new studies proving or disproving certain pedagogies, the media articles whipping up hysteria about the ways in which schools are failing, the marketing teams trying to sell the next new idea that will "revolutionise" education, the jostling for curriculum attention ("We should be teaching more of my this or that") and the politicians promising new policy directions that will solve this or that problem. Education is intense and it is noisy.

This book cannot quiet the noise and it does not try to pretend that teaching is easy. Teaching can be a deeply rewarding profession, but it is also extremely challenging at times. It is not made any easier by empty promises, overly simplistic solutions, or misleading catchphrases. There are, however, more and less intelligent ways to approach the job that can make those aspects of education within an individual teacher's control less burdensome and even enjoyable.

This cuts to the heart of the aim of this book: to provide a practical introduction for those beginning or preparing to teach history in secondary schools. The intended emphasis is on the "practical" (things that will help you begin to do the job with greater clarity and confidence) and it should be seen as a starting point rather than an exhaustive manual.

If there is an overarching argument of this book, it is to stress what Bob Bain suggested when he wrote that secondary history teachers must remain "bifocal by pursuing both *historical* and *instructional* lines of thinking".[1] Sole emphasis

---

1 Robert Bain, "'They Thought the World Was Flat?' Applying the Principles of How People Learn in Teaching High School History", in Donovan, S., and Bransford, J. (eds.) *How Students Learn: History in the Classroom*, National Academies Press, 2005, p. 182.

on the "historical" might provide a teacher with a sound scholarly basis for the content and ideas they foreground in their classes, but it may not translate into time well spent in class. A myopic focus on the "instructional" might, on the other hand, make for efficient classes in which students develop shallow or misleading ideas about history.

Teaching an unnatural act

This book begins from the basic premise, then, that because teaching secondary history is bifocal, it is unique in important respects. It is different to teaching physics, literature, industrial arts and physical education. To say that history is unique is to emphasise a notion that has a long pedigree. Many teachers and scholars have stressed that history requires distinctive modes of thinking that are, in many ways, "unnatural" to us as humans.[2]

Of course, there are many overlaps between the subjects in a typical school curriculum, but they are not identical, and they all have unique challenges. Both physics and history require students to make sense of evidence, for example, but the nature of that evidence is different, and it often requires different processes of evaluation, synthesis and communication.

The key focus in the book is, therefore, on outlining, explaining and modelling a range of different ideas that I think help solve problems common to history teaching in a wide variety of schools. All teachers have to plan units of work, but what are some unique strategies for planning a history unit? All teachers are required to develop assessment tasks, but what are some common errors to avoid in history? All teachers must provide feedback to students, but what is different about providing feedback on an extended piece of historical writing compared with mathematical working?

In doing this, much of what is outlined and discussed in this book is not new. In many ways, it openly and unashamedly tries to synthesise what I consider to be convincing and helpful conceptualisations of school history that have been influential in many parts of the world for some time.[3] The key project here is not to break new theoretical ground in thinking about history education, but to bring together important ideas in a book that can be read relatively quickly.

---

2 See Sam Wineburg, *Historical Thinking and Other Unnatural Acts: Charting the Future of Teaching the Past*, Temple University Press, 2001, and Peter Lee, "History Education and Historical Literacy", in Davies, I. (ed.) *Debates in History Teaching*, Routledge, 2017, pp. 55–65.
3 Arthur Chapman, "Historical Thinking/Historical Knowing: On the Content of the Form of History Education" in Counsell, C., Burn, K., and Chapman, A. (eds.) *Masterclass in History Education: Transforming Teaching and Learning*, Bloomsbury, 2016, pp. 225–31.

Theory and practice

Although this book does not aim to be a complete and systematic guide to teaching secondary history, I have also tried to ensure that, in emphasising the practical, more abstract and theoretical concerns are not entirely sidelined. Not only would this be dangerous, but it is also, to some degree, impossible since the line between the "purely theoretical" and the "purely practical" is not easy to demarcate when it comes to teaching history. Knowing how to teach a subject is, I would argue, bound up intimately with our perceptions of what the subject is, and what it is for.

The ideas presented here also try to build on a rich tradition of discussion around what useful teacher knowledge might be. In this I tend to agree with Barbara Duncan, who has perceptively claimed that:

> *Teacher knowledge is a messy kind of wisdom involving content knowledge, learning research, and teaching techniques as well as knowledge that can only be attained in social practice or by personal experimentation.*[4]

Work stretching back to Lee Shulman in the 1980s has also stressed the multifaceted nature of teacher knowledge and the symbiotic relationship between theoretical considerations and practical wisdom.[5]

So, in selecting the chapters, deciding on where emphases might be placed, and offering examples and anecdotes, I have tried to take seriously education research of various kinds (including specific research into history education), the applied research and reflections of practising history teachers, and my own experience in a variety of schools and educational settings. Collectively, I hope that, despite the necessary gaps in what can be covered in such a brief book, what emerges from these chapters is a practical orientation for both thinking *about* history education and beginning to teach the subject in schools.

Underlying assumptions

To maintain this tighter focus on history, I have had to be relatively ruthless in choosing what to place in the foreground, what to leave in the background,

---

4   Barbara Duncan, "On Teacher Knowledge: A Return to Shulman", *Philosophy of Education*, 1998: https://educationjournal.web.illinois.edu/archive/index.php/pes/article/view/2135.pdf
5   See Lee Shulman, "Knowledge and Teaching: Foundations of the New Reform", *Harvard Educational Review*, Vol. 57, No. 1, 1987, pp. 1-21, Lee Shulman, "Those Who Understand: Knowledge Growth in Teaching", *Educational Researcher*, Vol. 15, No. 2, 1986, pp. 4-14, and Barbara Duncan, "On Teacher Knowledge: A Return to Shulman", *Philosophy of Education*, 1998, pp. 378-80.

and what to eliminate altogether. To make these decisions a little more transparent, it is only fair to outline some of the key assumptions of this book that cannot be teased out in detail throughout the various chapters.

In the broadest sense, this book assumes that you have already developed, or are working on developing, a wider landscape of educational ideas that shape your knowledge and identity as a teacher. It assumes, for example, that you are working on developing a richer understanding of the insights provided by psychology for the purposes of teaching. This book does not, therefore, provide lengthy discussions about the brain, working and long-term memory, or specific themes such as neurodiversity and metacognition. These issues have been explored in-depth and by far more knowledgeable people to warrant repetition here.

In addition, I have almost entirely avoided specific discussions of key aspects of more general classroom craft that are essential to effective teaching. Most obviously, I say very little about classroom management in this book, despite the fact that none of the ideas outlined here would work in an unsafe or disorderly classroom environment. Again, since this is not a complete guide to teaching history, I assume that through teacher education courses, professional reading, collaboration and experience, you are already developing your confidence in these areas.

More-perceptive readers might also notice a range of assumptions underpinning this book regarding teachers, learning, students, history and education more generally. It would be impossible to lay all of these bare, but some of the more important ideas include:

- The notion that teachers play a crucial role in learning beyond simplistic notions of teacher- or student-centredness.
- A conviction that education is most powerful when, overall, it provides students with something beyond their natural and readily available resources. If schooling simply affirms what students already know and enjoy, then their ideas about the world and themselves are unlikely to be meaningfully expanded by the many hours they spend in classrooms, and we might be better off letting them do something else entirely.
- The view that teaching history in secondary schools should be fundamentally dynamic and adaptive. It should, within reasonable boundaries, move and shift as needed in different contexts. Sometimes those movements will be minor adjustments and at other times they will be much more significant.

- That teaching history is an important job. The "important" here means that I think it should be taken seriously and performed to the highest possible standard. The "job" here means that there should also be boundaries on what it demands of individuals.

The main context I had in mind while planning and writing this book was comprehensive secondary school settings. That is, schools from any sector that take in students with a range of prior achievement. In addition, the ideas I set out here are mainly for teaching core or mandatory history components of a curriculum in comprehensive contexts rather than elective, enrichment and extension components. Teaching history to Year 7 students in a comprehensive secondary school who have not chosen the subject is likely to present different challenges to teaching a small group of 15-year-old budding enthusiasts in an academically selective setting who have opted to take an elective history class. The tips presented here have the former setting in mind even though many are, I would argue, still worth considering in the latter. I also try to offer some discussion and examples relevant to teaching history in the senior years.

By now, I also hope that the tone of this book is becoming clear. It does not attempt to be definitive or make outlandish claims that it captures the "true path" to teaching secondary history. It does not try to debunk alternative approaches even though it makes arguments in favour of particular ideas.

Importantly, this book also tries to balance a sense of enthusiasm and high standards for the subject – an anti-mediocrity approach – with an anti-hero, anti-martyr message. More than ever, there seems to be a real danger in uncritically repeating the popular notion that education is "all about the students". In one sense that is obviously true, but, in another sense, it is a sentiment that can unintentionally encourage an unhealthy sense of self-sacrifice and place heavy burdens on teachers. Perhaps it would be better to say that education is "all about the community" (of students, teachers, administrators and families), since nothing works in isolation and a system full of burned-out teachers is ultimately no good to students anyway.

Using this book

The ideas and approaches in this book are squarely directed at early-career professionals who want some additional support as they set out on a path towards clarity, quality, enjoyment and growth as secondary history teachers. If you are looking for ammunition in a cosmic battle about how to fix education or the philosophy of history, you will need to look elsewhere.

The book is structured around three main overlapping parts, each including multiple chapters. Part One attempts to set out some foundational ideas about approaching secondary history in the early stages of your career. Parts Two and Three attempt to set out a range of suggestions for planning to teach. Part Two focuses on broad-level planning – topics, units, major assessment and so on – and Part Three focuses more on ideas relevant to smaller sequences and individual lessons.

Overall, I have opted to approach this book using a larger number of smaller chapters instead of fewer extended chapters. The main reason for breaking the content down into more bite-sized chapters was so that they can be read quickly and therein be more useful to teachers working full-time and pre-service teachers on practicum. Some chapters could also be useful as common readings in the context of teacher professional learning or university tutorials.

In addition to the ideas and arguments I have set out in the chapters, I have also included some suggestions for further reading, questions for your own reflection or discussion, and questions that you might ask a more experienced colleague such as a supervisor or head teacher. The suggestions for further readings try to point towards the rich thinking that already exists on most big questions of history education, while the questions will hopefully stimulate your own thinking about secondary history and also help to ground the ideas in the real experiences of teachers working in schools. I would not expect that every teacher's response to these questions would be identical or even in agreement with what I have argued in parts of this book, but that is part of the point: gaining confidence as a history teacher involves hearing different perspectives, observing different approaches in action, and ultimately forging your own professional approach within the boundaries of the system in which you teach.

As someone who loves history and history education, it really does make me happy that so many enthusiastic, intelligent and creative people choose to teach this crucial subject. My hope is that you will consider the ideas and tips presented here critically and, as your confidence grows, adapt, ignore and add to them as needed to forge your own professional path forward. In years to come, I hope that you will look back on these ideas, find value in what they gave you, but also see their limitations. For now, I hope this little book helps you start moving in a positive direction.

Further reading

Resource	Why bother reading it?
Lee Shulman, "Those Who Understand: Knowledge Growth in Teaching", *Educational Researcher*, Vol. 15, No. 2, 1986, pp. 4–14	This article from the 1980s sets out an interesting discussion of teacher expertise. Though his arguments have been contested, his emphasis on the importance of subject expertise is, in my view, helpful.
Tom Sherrington, *The Learning Rainforest: Great Teaching in Real Classrooms*, John Catt, 2017	Although Tom Sherrington is a science teacher, many of his ideas about teaching are useful for various subjects. This book offers a practical introduction to a key range of issues relating to teaching and I think it is worth reading in the early stages of your career to orientate yourself to a wide range of important issues, including curriculum, classroom management, assessment and more.
Robert Parkes, "Developing Your Approach to Teaching History", *Historical Thinking for History Teachers: A New Approach to Engaging Students and Developing Historical Consciousness*, Allen & Unwin, 2019, pp. 72–88	This chapter explores a range of key questions and issues that you will have to decide upon as you learn to teach secondary history.

Part One
Setting Foundations

CHAPTER 1

Take joy in the subject

Although I could hardly claim that the histories of Islam and north Africa are my specialties, I am fascinated by the 14th century scholar Ibn Khaldun (1332–1406 CE). I have long thought that the dramatic stories of his life and career surrounded by tragedy, political intrigue and an enduring quest for wisdom would make a wonderful film in the hands of the right director.[6] Ibn Khaldun was born in Tunis to an Andalusian family, lost his parents in a wave of the Black Death, worked in multiple governments across north Africa and Egypt, was imprisoned for conspiracy, wrote his most famous work in an isolated castle, lost his own family in a tragic shipwreck and, during the siege of Damascus (1400 CE), negotiated with the Turkic-Mongol ruler Tamerlane for safe passage of civilian workers before the city was violently sacked. What most interests me about Ibn Khaldun, however, is his writing on history.

Ibn Khaldun's most widely known work by far is the *Muqaddimah*, which was written as an extensive preface to a larger history of the Maghreb (north Africa) called the *Kitab al-Ibar*. In that preface, Ibn Khaldun discussed various ideas relating to the philosophy and practice of history as he saw it from his 14th century viewpoint. One of my favourite sections from that discussion is the opening passage of the foreword, which reads:

> *History is a discipline widely cultivated among nations and races. It is eagerly sought after. The men in the street, the ordinary people, aspire to know it. Kings and leaders vie for it.*
>
> *Both the learned and the ignorant are able to understand it. For on the surface history is no more than information about political events, dynasties, and occurrences of the remote past, elegantly presented and spiced with proverbs. It serves to entertain large, crowded gatherings and brings to us an understanding of human affairs. It shows how changing*

---

6 For an excellent and recent biography, see Robert Irwin, *Ibn Khaldun: An Intellectual Biography*, Princeton University Press, 2018.

conditions affected [human affairs], how certain dynasties came to occupy an ever wider space in the world, and how they settled the earth until they heard the call and their time was up.

The inner meaning of history, on the other hand, involves speculation and an attempt to get at the truth, subtle explanation of the causes and origins of existing things, and deep knowledge of the how and why of events. History, therefore, is firmly rooted in philosophy. It deserves to be accounted a branch of it.[7]

Despite obvious differences between our contexts and worldviews, and despite the fact that I recoil to some degree at aspects of the elitism in the comments, some of Ibn Khaldun's observations about history resonate with my own.

The appeal of history

First, the claim that history is "eagerly sought after" by many people ranging from "ordinary people" to "Kings and leaders". Though I cannot speak for the truth of that in the context of 14th century north Africa, I would certainly agree that history remains popular in the 21st century among wide audiences.[8] I cannot fully explain why, but I have little doubt that history enjoys a popular and powerful presence in many of our lives regardless of age, gender, class and educational background. That very point and the questions it raises fascinate me, particularly if it was also true of north Africa in the 14th century.

In addition, I agree with Ibn Khaldun that one appealing feature of history is the surface-level information that entertains and also seems to offer something in terms of understanding human affairs. I will freely admit that I enjoy and even seek out films, podcasts and easy-to-read articles and books that say little about the more analytical or philosophical layers of history but instead focus on telling powerful and interesting stories. There is wonder and even a degree of escapism in these stories of the past that capture parts of my imagination and I suspect this is a common reason for history's continuing popularity in many societies.

Then, there is what Ibn Khaldun calls the "inner meaning" of history: exploring "subtle explanations", poring over accounts that offer plausible reasons for the "how and why of events", all in an "attempt to get at the truth". Though at

---

7 Ibn Khaldun, *The Muqaddimah (Abridged Edition Translated by Franz Rosenthal)*, Princeton University Press, 2005, p. 5.
8 For a good example of this, see Roy Rosenzweig and David Thalen, *The Presence of the Past: Popular Uses of History in American Life*, Columbia University Press, 1998.

times this can be taxing, I also genuinely enjoy the intellectual challenge of reading through alternative narratives and arguments and reflecting on my own responses to different ways of interpreting the past. Many other people outside the historical profession appear to like this too – debating historical issues, hearing from different viewpoints and challenging ideas.

Finally, Ibn Khaldun makes an even larger claim: that history is rooted in "philosophy". Here we would do well to note the scholar Robert Irwin's claim that the reference to "philosophy" in this context is best translated not as the academic discipline of formal philosophy but as "wisdom" – gaining useful insights that help us as individuals and societies.[9] In other words, Ibn Khaldun was suggesting that history could be practical in orientating us to the world in which we live and the nature of the societies we belong to. I am sure that I would disagree with Khaldun on precisely what wisdom history can offer, but the fundamental argument that knowing something of the past is useful seems hard to deny. Attempting to figure out exactly what its use might be is all part of the joy of history in my view.

So, despite the fact that there is a danger in trying to make a 14th century Muslim scholar seem as though he was writing directly for a 21st century multicultural audience, I do think many of the points Ibn Khaldun raised about history still resonate in the modern world. Moreover, I would go further and suggest that aspects of what he appears to be claiming about the nature and appeal of history stand broadly true for the subject in contemporary secondary school settings.

The appeal of history in schools

In my experience, many students do (or come to) enjoy the "surface level" aspects of history – the stories, the characters, the strangeness of past worlds and, at times, their surprising familiarity. Many, when taught well, also come to enjoy exploring history's "inner meaning". In fact, students often report that some of the most enjoyable aspects of school history are those opportunities to discuss, debate and contest the past (of course in an environment of safety and respect).[10]

As we begin to explore some foundational ideas for the teaching of history in schools, it is important that we begin with what we enjoy about the subject

---

9 Robert Irwin, *Ibn Khaldun: An Intellectual Biography*, Princeton University Press, 2018, pp. 65–70.
10 See, for example, Anna Clark, "Teaching and Learning Difficult Histories" in Epstein, T. and Peck, C. (eds.) *Teaching and Learning Difficult Histories in International Contexts: A Critical Sociocultural Approach*, Routledge, 2019, pp. 82–94.

and what our students might enjoy too. To be sure, there are times when a topic we are required to teach may not excite us or our students terribly much. Some students might find aspects of studying the past challenging emotionally or intellectually and so resist. But, in an age when secondary teaching has become more bureaucratic, technocratic and procedural than ever, I think it is fundamentally important to remember what it is about this subject that we love and what might have most appeal for our students. One of the great advantages of history as a school subject is its potential for wide and varied interest.

In a 2016 study conducted on student perceptions of teacher authenticity, Pedro de Bruyckere and Paul Kirschner found that a "passionate teacher can have a 'contagious' effect on the pupils". Interestingly, they went on to add that "This is very different than more 'Rousseau-based' views on education that put an emphasis on the passions of the pupils to be followed and supported by their teachers".[11] Though I would not discount student interest as an important feature of education, experience certainly suggests that teacher interest and passion can also contribute to positive learning experiences for many young people.

Lest my point be misunderstood, I am not at all suggesting that we should try to turn history into an entertainment club or that we should artificially present an obsessive or disingenuous enthusiasm for our subject. My claim is that we will give ourselves far greater chance of satisfaction and success as history teachers if we consider what it is that makes our subject appealing to ourselves and the students we teach. For me, that enthusiasm lies in some of the ideas hinted at by Ibn Khaldun, but there is much more to it than that too.

Chapter summary

- People appear to be fascinated by different aspects of history which can all be used in secondary teaching.
- Stories, characters, historical debates, and the philosophy of history can all pique student (and teacher) interest in different ways.
- It is important to reflect on what it is about history that you like as a teacher and consider what aspects of history your students are most interested by too.

---

11 Pedro de Bruyckere, Paul Kirschner and Yvonne Xian-han Huang, "Authentic Teachers: Student Criteria Perceiving the Authenticity of Teachers", *Cogent Education*, Vol. 3, No. 1, 2016, pp. 1–15.

End of chapter questions

Questions for reflection and discussion	Questions to ask experienced teachers
1. What do you enjoy about history? 2. What got you interested in history? 3. Examine the history curriculum that you will be required to teach in your jurisdiction. What aspects do you find most interesting? Are there aspects that you think might be harder to enjoy than others?	1. What aspects of the curriculum do you think students respond most readily to? 2. Are there aspects of history (skills, etc.) that students find more interesting than others? 3. How do you keep your enjoyment of history alive as you teach?

Further reading

Resource	Why bother reading it?
Jonathon Dallimore, "History" in Sharp, H., et. al. *Teaching Secondary History*, Cambridge University Press, 2021, pp. 3–25	This chapter provides a broad overview of the history of history as a discipline. It also provides some ways of thinking about history as a public and popular pursuit which have important implications for secondary history.
Suzannah Lipscomb and Helen Carr (eds.), *What is History Now? How the Past and Present Speak to Each Other*, Weidenfeld and Nicolson, 2022	This book provides excellent and interesting scholarship on the state of the discipline in the 21st century. It builds on other titles of the same or similar name that can also be useful resources for thinking about history and the way it has (and has not) changed over time.

CHAPTER 2

Value and nurture your subject expertise

Subject knowledge is a crucial dimension of secondary history teachers' work. Unfortunately, this is not as valued as it should be in modern education where the focus of staff meetings and in-school professional learning sometimes feels as though it is on everything *but* subject knowledge.

Not only does stronger and deeper subject knowledge increase the likelihood that your teaching is more robust, it makes the day-to-day work easier. It seems obvious to note it, but if your subject knowledge is shallow, it is much harder to make useful connections between themes and topics, harder to conduct productive class discussions, more time-consuming to filter through or create resources, harder to challenge students in appropriate ways, and difficult to provide them with meaningful feedback likely to improve their performance in key areas of the subject. Weak subject knowledge can be a serious drag on many aspects of teaching.

Of course, as noted in the introduction to this book, the insights of Lee Shulman remind us that this does not mean that subject knowledge is sufficient to make anyone an effective teacher.[12] Knowing more and more about history cannot magically give you the ability to work effectively with students, but the absence of strong subject knowledge is almost guaranteed to place clear limits on your teaching.

Subject knowledge beyond the curriculum

In her book *Teaching to the Top: Aiming High for Every Learner* (2021), Megan Mansworth places subject knowledge at the foundation of teaching.

---

12 Lee Shulman, "Knowledge and Teaching: Foundations of the New Reform", *Harvard Educational Review*, Vol. 57, No. 1, 1987, pp. 1–21.

She suggests, correctly in my view, that teachers should not simply aim to know "just enough" to cover their lessons, but should aspire to a deeper level of expertise and confidence with their subject. She writes: "It is much easier to learn at a higher level than the one you need to teach at and work backwards from there, than to learn only to the level of the scheme of learning or curriculum point in question".[13]

There are certainly times when this is difficult, especially in the early stages of your career when you are often teaching topics for the first time. There are also situations in which knowing just enough will be sufficient to get you through a few lessons, and that is perfectly acceptable. That kind of teaching is, however, probably more about survival than ultimate aspiration.

It is also important to remember that you may not need the same depth of knowledge for every topic you teach. For example, if you only teach Ancient Greece to Year 7 as a 5-week overview topic, your subject knowledge for that topic will not need to be as deep as it will need to be if you teach a 10-week intensive unit on the Peloponnesian Wars at senior level.

Overall, however, rich and confident subject knowledge as a secondary history teacher not only helps to improve the quality of your teaching but also makes many aspects of the job easier and more enjoyable. It will, for example, have at least some influence on aspects of teaching outlined in Table 2.1.

TABLE 2.1: How subject knowledge can make teaching history easier and more enjoyable

The degree to which you enjoy teaching	If you do not enjoy the subject(s) you teach, teaching will fast become a tedious chore. If you do enjoy your subject, as I think most secondary history teachers do, richer knowledge of the subject is likely to enhance your own enthusiasm. This can include deepening one's knowledge of topics one is familiar with, or moving into new areas that broaden and enrich one's historical understanding.
Your confidence	Deeper knowledge of the discipline and the topics you teach more specifically allows you to approach planning, teaching and assessment with greater composure. It also means that you can be more agile and responsive when problems arise.

---

[13] Megan Mansworth, *Teaching to the Top: Aiming High for Every Learner,* John Catt Educational, 2021, p. 19.

The quality of your instruction	A teacher with excellent classroom management skills and deep knowledge of cognitive science might be an efficient teacher, but poor subject knowledge may mean that they pass on errors and problems that will need to be fixed later. Deeper knowledge can make quality planning faster, resourcing quicker, feedback on student work more targeted, and so on.
Your ability to connect your students to the subject	Greater subject knowledge makes it much easier to find interesting narratives, lines of questioning, resources and anecdotes that can enliven the subject for students.

Subject knowledge that rises above the baseline of what is required to get through lessons also improves the conceptual quality of your teaching. Wider knowledge allows you to be clearer, both to yourself and to the students, about what might be distinctive and significant about the topics and themes you explore. For example, if you are required to teach about a major battle on the Western Front during the First World War, it helps to know about other battles too, even if you are not required to explore them in depth. Richer knowledge of the conflict as a whole will enable you to train attention on the most unique and interesting aspects of the battle you are required to focus on.

Sometimes, I explain this as the ability to "see the whole and the parts". If, in the example above, you constrain your knowledge to the single battle from the First World War that you must teach about, you are likely to miss many opportunities because your sense of the whole is lacking. If, however, you have a strong working knowledge of the broader features of the conflict and a range of other battles (the whole), this will sharpen your knowledge of the battle (the part) because you can place it in a broader context and highlight key themes and details that help capture its distinct qualities. I think my confidence is at its peak when I have a strong knowledge of the whole and the parts that I am working with, and this usually requires knowledge beyond the baseline requirements of the curriculum.

Consolidating and expanding subject knowledge

Expanding your subject knowledge so that it sits comfortably above the baseline requirements of the curriculum you are teaching takes time, and it can be hard work. It is not a short-term objective but a career-long aspiration. It seems to be the case, however, that the more subject knowledge you develop, the quicker it becomes to expand and refine.

When asked by early career teachers how to work on this content knowledge, the simple answer I offer is to start moving and plan for incremental growth.

Too much agonising over strategies and too much deliberating about what to read next can grind to an unproductive halt. So, spend some time considering what you are required to teach, think about which area(s) you feel least confident in, and begin working on those.

More specifically, I think it can be helpful to plan to expand your subject knowledge through different strategies. And so I ask:

- What should I read? Entire books are excellent, and I tend to start with an overall narrative history if I am teaching a topic for the first time. For example, if I am teaching the Cold War, I will look for a well-reviewed history of that conflict and read it from cover to cover. I usually then try to read some more specific interpretations around key questions from the topic.
- What should I attend? Your local subject association should provide professional learning that will help build your subject and pedagogical knowledge. Attending online or face-to-face workshops, lectures and teachers' study sessions will help you develop confidence in areas in which you currently feel unsure.
- What should I watch? Search for good documentaries covering the topics you teach. Not only are these informative for you, but you can often use these in classrooms with students too. I also like to watch historical films, not to learn the facts of the topic, but to see how aspects of history have been creatively interpreted. This can provide helpful talking points too if the students have also seen the film.
- What should I listen to? Podcasts and other programs can be cheap and relatively quick ways to build your subject knowledge. There are a range of brilliant podcasts hosted by professional historians. *Empire* by William Dalrymple and Anita Anand and *New Books in History* have some excellent episodes.
- What should I visit? I think it is crucial that secondary history teachers explore history as it is presented in public. This includes finding monuments, visiting museums, and travelling to historic sites where possible. These can be informative and also provide useful anecdotes and images for use in the classroom with students.

It is important to remember that not all your reading, listening and visiting will result immediately in predictable and concrete "resources" for your classes. Sometimes when reading I take notes with a plan to share these with students, for example, but other times I just read to expand my knowledge. In the very least, expanding one's knowledge should help to expand one's appreciation of history and one's general disciplinary knowledge, but it can also inform and inspire your teaching in unexpected ways. I am often surprised how anecdotes and stories from books I have read, films I have watched, and places I have visited come to mind mid-discussion with a class. When used carefully and constructively, these can help clarify and enliven lessons, and the spontaneity can even help to keep teaching (dare I say it?) fun.

DIAGRAM 2.1: Consuming history for general and concrete purposes

← **General and personal** | **Concrete and immediate** →

Consume history because you enjoy it and it brings value to your life, not just because you are required to somehow transmit it to other people for work. Read books because you enjoy them, watch films and documentaries because they inform or stir your imagination, visit museums and sites because being in the presence of the past can be a fascinating experience.

Consume history because it gives you more material to work with in the classroom. The additional knowledge gained from reading a good book on a topic you must teach is likely to give you more ideas for how to teach the material. This should be the same for visiting sites, watching films and documentaries and engaging with history in any of the ways it is available to use in the modern world.

Much of the knowledge and insight that you gain from consuming history as you teach will not predictably impact your teaching. You may not get a photograph, a collection of notes or new primary sources to share with the class. It is likely, however, that it will begin to indirectly shape your teaching or be used in unpredictable ways. For example, visiting a site might give you a body of anecdotes that you use spontaneously and reading a book might dramatically improve spontaneous answers that you give to questions in class.

Consuming history for yourself is worthwhile because it contributes to:

- Your enjoyment of the world.
- Your general disciplinary awareness of the different ways in which history is conceived and produced.
- Your awareness of what exists and what is possible.
- Your personal identity by learning about key traditions, ideas, patterns of life, etc.

Consuming history for your work in classrooms can be productive:

- As you read books or articles, collate brief notes that can be shared with the class to provide new insights into topics you teach.
- Where appropriate, take good photographs of historic sites and exhibits to use in the classroom to illustrate key ideas within lessons.
- Gather stories, descriptions of space/locations and anecdotes that can enliven your teaching.

First nations histories

In contexts such as Australia, Canada and the United States, it is crucial as a history teacher to ensure that part of your subject expertise includes the histories of First Nations peoples. Not only is this a dimension of history often foregrounded by curriculum, but deep knowledge and understanding of these aspects of history can contribute to what Treesa Heath calls "authentic reconciliation education".[14]

In Australia, this particularly includes exploring the rich and complex histories of First Nations peoples in deep time and more recent contexts. Fortunately, there are a growing number of excellent resources for teachers and students that facilitate this.[15]

Chapter summary

- Subject knowledge is a foundational aspect of secondary history teaching, and it should be prioritised.
- Not only does subject knowledge help to ensure that your teaching is more effective, but it can also make teaching easier and more enjoyable.
- Developing subject knowledge takes time and can be challenging, especially in your early career.
- Consider different strategies for expanding your subject knowledge such as reading, listening, viewing and visiting.
- Subject knowledge can help produce specific and concrete resources for teaching, but it can also feed into spontaneous stories, anecdotes and illustrations that enliven your lessons in unpredictable ways.
- In contexts such as Australia, New Zealand, Canada and the United States, a crucial aspect of subject knowledge that should be prioritised is that of First Nations histories.

---

14 Treesa Heath, "Aboriginal and Torres Strait Islander Histories and Cultures", *Teaching Secondary History*, Cambridge University Press, 2021, p. 209.
15 See, for example, HTANSW, *Ancient Australia: An Introductory Guide for Teachers and Students*, History Teachers' Association of New South Wales, 2024.

End of chapter questions

Questions for reflection and discussion	Questions to ask experienced teachers
1. In what ways does subject knowledge empower teaching? 2. Why is it important to aspire to develop subject knowledge that goes beyond the baseline requirements of the curriculum you teach? 3. What are your preferred ways of consuming history and expanding your knowledge? Are there new suggestions provided in this chapter that you could also try?	1. How do you develop your subject knowledge when you are required to teach a new topic for the first time? 2. How do you keep your subject knowledge updated and fresh?

Further reading

Resource	Why bother reading it?
Suzannah Lipscomb and Helen Carr (eds.), *What Is History Now? How the Past and Present Speak to Each Other*, Weidenfeld and Nicolson, 2022	This book provides excellent and interesting scholarship on the state of the discipline in the 21st century. It builds on other titles of the same or similar name that can also be useful resources for thinking about history and the way it has (and has not) changed over time.
Megan Mansworth, *Teaching to the Top: Aiming High for Every Learner*, John Catt Educational, 2021 (Chapter 1: "Building the Foundations: Developing High-Level Subject Knowledge")	The first chapter of this book offers a refreshing discussion that places a teacher's subject knowledge and expertise at the centre of their teaching. Not only does this assist in teaching effectively, but it also nurtures a teacher's own enthusiasm for teaching. It is a good reminder that teaching should not simply be seen as a technocratic delivery process and that the ends are at least as important as the means.

Resource	Why bother reading it?
Treesa Heath, "Aboriginal and Torres Strait Islander Histories and Cultures", *Teaching Secondary History*, Port Melbourne: Cambridge University Press, 2021, pp. 203–226	Treesa Heath offers considered and practical ideas about approaching First Nations histories in an Australian context. She also discusses some important pedagogical considerations for teaching indigenous students, along with some excellent resources that teachers might consult.
Kay Traille, ""Common sense" and Issues of Social Justice in History Education", *The History Teacher*, Vol. 56, No. 3, 2023, pp. 319–341	Traille's article challenges history teachers to think deeply about the positions and perspective from and through which history is taught and learned.
Ann McGrath, "What is Deep History", *Teaching History*, Vol. 56, No. 1, 2022, pp. 4–8	This article provides a brief and clear introduction to key aspects of deep time history with a focus on an Australian context.

CHAPTER 3

Develop a vision for why you teach history

In a chapter contributed to the book *Debates in History Teaching* (2017), Peter Lee argued that history teachers:

> ... *must escape the tyranny of tasks and algorithmic "methods". Teachers must have aims and objectives beyond the "successful" completion of a classroom task. Any task (however good) can in itself only be a step towards something bigger. It must fit into a wider conception of what history education is trying to do... "Completing the task" can never be an adequate statement of objectives let alone aims.*[16]

If you have decided to teach secondary history, you probably already have some idea of what you think history education is for. You might believe that history holds some keys to understanding the present that you want to share with others. You might believe that it is possible for humans (and humanity) to "learn from the past". You might even think that learning history has the power to make people more active and ethical citizens of their communities.

Most curriculum documents will already include some attempts to justify the study of history. Common among these are that it helps students appreciate the broader contexts surrounding their contemporary world, develops reasoned or critical thinking, and encourages active democracy.

These reasons are all generally noble, but it is important from the outset to recognise that, just as knowledge of the past is contested, so are the reasons for teaching the subject. There are indeed logical grounds, for example, to challenge the notion that we can or do really "learn from the past". It is fair to question whether a knowledge of history really guarantees that someone will become an ethical participant in their community. And it could be

---

16 Peter Lee, "History Education and Historical Literacy" in Davies, I. (ed.) *Debates in History Teaching*, Routledge, 2017, p. 55.

considered naïve to think that history alone helps students develop a critical outlook on their world or that it is the only subject that helps them argue and communicate about abstract ideas.

So, a foundational challenge in teaching secondary history is to appreciate the arguments of others regarding the value of history, and to go a step further to develop your own convictions about history's worth in secondary schools.

Common reasons offered to justify history's value

There are many reasonably common explanations given for history's significance within a school curriculum. For ease of reference, we might call these patriotic, present, practical and political arguments, but these labels are far from comprehensive. Some of these are outlined in Table 3.1.

TABLE 3.1: Common reasons offered for the importance of history in schools

Patriotic	There are what we might call "hard" and "soft" versions of the patriotic defence of history as a subject. The harder version might appear to be nationalistic where someone promotes the idea that students should know history so that they can be uncritically proud of the great achievements of their nation. Softer versions may still argue that history should develop a sense of pride in one's nation albeit through a critical lens.
Present	It is common to argue that history is valuable because it helps students develop a broad orientation to the present in which they live by understanding the major developments in the national and global past. This view may be more agnostic as to whether students need to develop a sense of pride in their nation. It is more concerned with helping students make some sense of important aspects of the society in which they currently live.
Practical	As aspects of the previous discussion have already alluded to, some people argue that history has many practical qualities as a subject. Students consolidate deeper reading skills, they practise the art of analysing and synthesising information, they learn to research, they develop more sophisticated communication skills, they learn to think critically, and more. There is much truth to these claims, and a student who thrives in school history is likely to have developed knowledge and skills that will be helpful in many other settings.

Political	There are many claims about the political importance of history. Learning history in order to become unquestioningly proud of one's country, for example, is fundamentally a political suggestion, just as it would be political to claim that the purpose of history is to learn to unquestioningly detest one's country. But there are other arguments about the political importance of history. For example, it is often said that history can help students participate more effectively in democracy or that it helps them develop a sense of their "civic responsibilities". In Australia, the idea of civics education is often woven into history content. Even stronger claims might suggest that history can contribute to greater social justice and progress if it is taught appropriately and well. In contexts such as Australia, New Zealand, Canada and the United States, this often also includes visions for reconciliation and truth telling.

Intrinsic arguments for the value of history

Currently, when I am asked why someone should bother with history, I simply begin with the argument that I think it is fascinating. Like many others, I am genuinely intrigued by the stories and the people that we often study in history, and I am stimulated by the kinds of thinking that the discipline foregrounds: questions about causation, proof and evidence, perspective and change and continuity. I also enjoy the philosophy of history: thinking about how we claim to know about the past, how and why different people remember the past in various ways, what history is ultimately capable of, and so on. I think this curiosity and fascination drive my enthusiasm for studying and teaching the subject, and I have often thought that even if I did not work in history education I would still read, think about, and perhaps even write about the past.

History, I would argue, can also provide an important and profound window into the species, *Homo sapiens*, that I happen to be part of. Learning about my own national history has helped me understand the country that I call home, and this is a helpful orientation to the world in which I currently live. Learning about people who have lived in vastly different times and cultures has also given me a much wider appreciation of how members of my species have lived and tried to make sense of the world. All of this has helped to create small holes in the "windowless room of the present".[17]

---

17 David Harlan quoted in Herman Paul, "The Windowless Room of the Present: Rereading David Harlan", *Journal of the Philosophy of History*, Vol. 15, No. 3, 2021, p. 396.

Perhaps a little more philosophically, I also believe that there is great merit in what the English history educator Christine Counsell suggested about history when she wrote:

> *Some might say, "surely in school history, we can just teach the facts and leave disciplinary understanding until later?" But that would be both impossible and dangerous. For while many individual facts are known incontrovertibly, even to juxtapose two facts is to create a story. The interpretive process is brought to bear in the very generalizations we make, in the facts selected or ignored in each story. To leave children ignorant of how that interpretive process works, both the legitimate reasons why respectable accounts will vary and be provisional and the pernicious reasons for deliberately deceptive stories, would be irresponsible. Even if we could somehow find an objective, neutral collection of facts, a convenient canon on which everyone agreed, the idea that we might fool students until they were, say, 16, and do the difficult stuff later, is dangerous. Only a minority of students will study history post-16. The task facing a modern education system in a democracy is to ensure that no one leaves schools unaware that any story is a set of choices and carries a message, witting or unwitting.*[18]

In a society awash in the past, histories are everywhere and Counsell's observations seem crucial. Politicians of all persuasions mobilise national history to stir division or justify particular policies, filmmakers send public perceptions about the past off in new directions, interest groups lobby the government for curriculum change, and teachers are often left at the end of the line. Make no mistake, histories are not neutral. I am convinced that it helps to be aware of this and to be able to begin engaging thoughtfully with histories because it might shape your voting, your reaction to policy changes, your professional choices, and your own sense of identity.

Notice that these three comments on history's value have not strayed much beyond history itself. That is, they are all intrinsic arguments about the value of history. It is hard to realise any of the aims I have set out without deep knowledge of history. This, I think, begins to demonstrate that the subject has powerful justifications for its place in the curriculum *on its own*.

---

[18] Christine Counsell, "History" in Sehgal Cuthbert, A., and Standish, A. (eds.) *What Should Schools Teach? Disciplines, Subjects and the Pursuit of Truth (2nd Ed.)*, UCL Press, 2021, p. 156.

Extrinsic arguments for the value of history

There are, in my view, also good reasons to think that history has value beyond itself – sometimes called extrinsic reasons for its value. To take one general example, I am convinced that a good extrinsic argument for the value of history is offered by Sam Wineburg in *Why Study History? When It's Already on Your Phone* (2018), where he writes that good history: "... provides an antidote to impulse by cultivating modes of thought that counteract haste and avert premature judgment".[19] Wineburg also believes that history has intrinsic value, but I think this point is also profound. Sometimes I use the expression "good history is slow history" to capture the spirit of what I think Wineburg was trying to suggest here. History is a discipline that has made me think deeply about my own beliefs and about the way I arrive at them. I think it has slowed me down in an imperfectly positive sense, and that is something of value I would like others to benefit from. This is a general theme also taken up, though in a more technical manner, in popular works of psychology such as Daniel Kahneman's *Thinking Fast and Slow* (2011).

We might go a step further and, like Kenneth Nordgren, argue that history also has much of value to contribute to "real world" contemporary concerns.[20] Importantly, this does not require school history to lose sight of its disciplinary foundations and integrity. If E. H. Carr's assertion that history is an "unending dialogue between the present and the past" is accurate, Nordgren reminds us that it would be unwise to pretend that history should "only be occupied with keeping its distance from contemporary culture".[21] It might give students something of value to work with when they confront the Anthropocene, the alleged weakening of modern democracy, and other key challenges prominent in the 21st century.

At this point we might begin to think of a raft of reasons that history is valuable beyond itself. It teaches research skills, the ability to handle complex ideas, comfort with uncertainty, creativity, criticality, and so on. Personally, however, I begin to tread very carefully from here because, as Michael Fordham has argued, it is entirely possible that we will run into a messy set

---

19 Sam Wineburg, *Why Learn History? When It's Already on Your Phone*, University of Chicago Press, 2018, p. 7.
20 Kenneth Nordgren, "Powerful Knowledge for What? History Education and 45-degree Discourse" in Chapman, A. (ed.) *Knowing History in Schools: Powerful Knowledge and the Powers of Knowledge*, UCL Press, 2021, pp. 177–201.
21 Kenneth Nordgren, "Powerful Knowledge for What? History Education and 45-degree Discourse" in Chapman, A. (ed.) *Knowing History in Schools: Powerful Knowledge and the Powers of Knowledge*, UCL Press, 2021, p. 194.

of ideas.[22] If, for example, we argue that history is valuable *only* or *primarily* because it teaches something general called "critical thinking", we may have unintentionally devalued the subject. I am certain that good science, English and design teaching can also inculcate critical thinking, so what then is the competitive value of history? If some generic idea of critical thinking is the aim, then it might be that traditional philosophy should be the only subject required in schools.

So, there clearly is a reasonable case to be made that history can and should play a significant role in our lives and that it has value beyond "knowing about the past". My personal preference is to lay initial, but not sole, emphasis on the intrinsic explanations for the subject's value and move from there.

A word of caution

This is all wonderful to reflect on and explore, but we also need to remember that, as secondary history teachers, we may not realise all of these aims with every student we teach, and that is perfectly acceptable. We need to be careful that we do not let our enthusiasm place an unachievable burden on what we can do with the limited time and resources we have in schools.

Some students we teach will go on to develop a genuine love for history and some may study it further. Others might never realise the full value of history while they are studying with us, but we need not feel deflated by this. We certainly do not want to over-promise and under-deliver what the subject *must* do for all students. Knowing the full scope of the subject's value, however, helps us see the possibilities, and this is a crucial start in preparing us to teach students with a wide range of experiences and interests.

In addition, although there is likely to be overlap in the way that many teachers justify the importance of history in schools, we should also expect some disagreement. That is not a sign of the subject's weakness, but rather a sign that it remains alive, so we should never try to shut down debate about what makes this subject valuable.

The important point is to have at least thought about why you believe teaching and studying history is worthwhile and important. This is likely to help sustain you when you lose sight of your purpose or feel overwhelmed by the drudgery of some questionable administrative burden that creeps into education from time to time.

---

22 Michael Fordham, "Genericism and the Crisis of Curriculum", 18 June 2016: https://clioetcetera.com/2016/06/18/genericism-and-the-crisis-of-curriculum/

Chapter summary

- There are many common arguments offered to justify the study of history in schools, but these are contested.
- Intrinsic arguments for the value of history focus on the subject itself and not a secondary goal such as generic "critical thinking" (though this has its place too).
- Developing a personal sense of why you believe that studying history is important will help clarify your purpose as a teacher and sustain you when the work inevitably gets tough.

End of chapter questions

Questions for reflection and discussion	Questions to ask experienced teachers
1. Review the reasons for valuing history outlined in this chapter. Which do you find the most/least convincing? 2. Can you think of other arguments that you would stress in attempting to explain the importance of history in secondary school?	1. What motivated you to teach history? 2. How do you explain the value of history to students and their parents? 3. How have your views about history changed since you began teaching?

Further reading

Resource	Why bother reading it?
Sam Wineburg, *Why Learn History? When It's Already on Your Phone*, University of Chicago Press, 2018	This book offers interesting arguments about the purpose of teaching history in an age when students can access so much information quickly.
Kay Traille, "'Common sense' and Issues of Social Justice in History Education", *The History Teacher*, Vol. 56, No. 3, 2023, pp. 319–41	Traille's article challenges history teachers to think deeply about the positions and perspectives from and through which history is taught and learned.
Peter Lee, "History Education and Historical Literacy", in Davies, I. (ed.) *Debates in History Teaching*, Routledge, 2017, pp. 55–65	In this chapter, Peter Lee offers a broad discussion of what history education in schools might aim to achieve. One key part of his answer is that "historical literacy" should be a fundamental goal of secondary history.

Resource	Why bother reading it?
Christopher Martell and Kaylene Stevens, *Teaching History for Justice: Centring Activism in Students' Understanding of the Past*, Columbia University Teachers' College Press, 2021	Martell and Stevens offer a more radical outlook for teaching history, suggesting that it can be explored through and for social justice lenses.
Keith Barton and Linda Levstik, *Teaching History for the Common Good*, Lawrence Erlbaum Associates, 2004	Barton and Levstik survey various justifications for teaching history and also argue that collaboration towards common goals should be central.
Harry Brighouse, "Should We Teach Patriotic History" in Curren, R. (ed.) *Philosophy of Education: An Anthology*, Blackwell Publishing, 2007, pp. 528–38	Harry Brighouse provides a critical discussion of patriotism and its relationship to school history.
Michael Stephen Schiro, *Curriculum Theory: Conflicting Visions and Enduring Concerns (2nd Ed.)*, Sage, 2013: Chapter 1: "Introduction to Curriculum Ideologies", pp. 1–14	Chapter 1 of Schiro's book outlines a range of general approaches to curriculum that will help make broader sense of some of the ideas in this chapter. He would suggest that I am mostly making a "Scholar Academic" argument for history in the curriculum.

CHAPTER 4

Treat history as a holistic process

In his book *Biology Made Real: Ways of Teaching that Inspire Meaning-Making* (2023), Christian Moore-Anderson wonders about learning by asking:

> *Can we say a student has understood a concept if we isolate it from everything else? Can we say a student understands the digestive system if they can detail the steps in the process, but cannot elaborate on why some animals have digestive systems in the first place? Do students simply need to* know *lots of things in biology? Or is there something deeper? Something students can improve upon all the way through secondary school that isn't simply accruing, or trying to remember, knowledge? What lies beyond the content itself?*[23]

As a science and languages teacher, Moore-Anderson believes there is, and he explains how he moved from a view of biology primarily focused on cells to one focused on organisms. Although cells are clearly important to understanding biology, in Moore-Anderson's view, the organism is a much more meaningful "hub" of connections that helps generate interesting and broader connections in biology. For Moore-Anderson, this also encourages students to ask meaningful questions that have bearing on their lives and identities. These include: What am I (or what kind of organism am I)? How did I come to be? Who were my ancestors? And how should I live with other organisms?

Though biology and history are quite different subjects involving exploration of unique questions, data and, often, forms of communication, this is a useful reminder that atomised learning in any subject can quickly become overwhelming and tedious. If we think of teaching history as just remembering a long run of facts, testing sources for their reliability or value,

---

[23] Christian Moore-Anderson, *Biology Made Real: Ways of Teaching that Inspire Meaning-Making* (Kindle), Self-published, 2023, p. 9.

and writing endless paragraphs of words, we run the risk of losing sight of the beauty of history's questions and the role the subject might play in our lives beyond the classroom. The discipline is not there just to help us remember facts, but to help us make sense of our individual and collective experiences across time.

But what might be a meaningful "hub" to frame history around? Is there something we can focus attention on if we are to teach history in a less atomised and more meaningful way?

I would argue that there is no single "unit of study" that can prevent history becoming too atomised such as Moore-Anderson's move from the cell to organism in biology. Framing history as the study of individuals, nations, periods, regions and even the species as a whole are all helpful at different times, but none of them should be the primary lens through which we explore the past.

Instead, like many others, I would suggest that framing history as a process of inquiry is a helpful way of preventing atomisation. It helps us place the many "parts" of working with history, such as narratives, questions, facts, evidence, argumentation and others, into a workable "whole" that can be adapted for smaller and larger scales of learning. The process of inquiry can be sped up and slowed down depending on student needs and the demands of time, and it can be tightly controlled by the teacher or opened up to allow for greater student freedom when appropriate.

History as a process of inquiry

The word history "... originally meant inquiry, the act of seeking knowledge, as well as the knowledge that results from inquiry".[24] This is, however, still vague since many disciplines investigate, "seek knowledge", and test the "results of inquiry". More specifically, we might think of history as a discipline interested in inquiring into the way humans have lived in different times and places, why they have lived in those ways, and how and why patterns of life have (or have not) changed over time.

Unfortunately, because the word "inquiry" has many meanings and has been used in various ways in education, it is often assumed that any learning framed through inquiry means something like "discovery learning", where students might be left to figure out solutions to problems without any teacher guidance. In school history, this is rarely the underlying idea when the term

---

24 Katy Steinmetz, "This Is Where the Word 'History' Comes From", *Time Magazine*, 23 June 2017: https://time.com/4824551/history-word-origins/

is used, and it is certainly not the fundamental idea presented in this book. As Lindsay Gibson and James Miles explain: "Effective inquiry is not defined by the degree to which inquiry is teacher- or student-directed, but by the quality of thinking that students exhibit".[25]

So, a better way to think of inquiry in the context of this book and of secondary history more generally is as a process of exploring stories and questions, finding and examining meaningful data, and presenting narratives and conclusions so that they can be discussed, challenged and adapted if necessary. Notice that this has nothing to do with how this process will be managed or conducted; it is not a pedagogical point but a conceptual point. In other words, inquiry in this context simply refers to a process of meaningful learning in which the parts all play a logical role in a larger whole. These parts are outlined in brief in Table 4.1.

TABLE 4.1: Key elements of the historical inquiry process

Questions and stories	Questions drive history. They give us something interesting to focus on, something clear to explore, and something to discuss and contest. How did early cities emerge? Why did Buddhism succeed as a world religion? Why was Napoleon so successful? How did the Bolshevik Revolution of 1917 end up in Stalinist nightmare? Why was the Roman Empire so powerful? Why have many modern societies built more statues to men than women?
	Often questions are difficult to separate from the stories we tell about the past and the knowledge we develop. It is not uncommon, for example, that students will raise many of these questions themselves as their knowledge of a topic expands.
Finding and analysing meaningful data	We cannot answer questions about the past without finding meaningful information that we can depend on. We often just refer to this as evidence, but it plays a crucial role in debates about the past. Often historians, politicians and everyday people disagree on facts and/or how they should be interpreted, and this leads to important differences in the conclusions many people draw. The ability to find and then intelligently and cautiously sift through enormous amounts of information is clearly one of the great challenges of the modern information age.

---

25 Lindsay Gibson and James Miles, "Inquiry Doesn't Just Happen" in Case, R., and Clark, P. (eds.) *Learning to Inquire in History, Geography and Social Studies: An Anthology for Secondary Teachers (4th Ed.)*, The Critical Thinking Consortium, 2020, p. 156.

Communicating, sharing and challenging stories and arguments	History is not simply questions and data; it is an interpretative discipline intensely interested in the stories told and the arguments developed about the past. In many ways, history is a competition between differing stories and arguments. Some people tell the story of the Second World War as though it started in 1939 when Germany invaded Poland, whereas others are adamant a better framing would begin in 1937 with Japan's invasion of China. Some people believe that the stories of Great Men explain the past, whereas others believe that everyday people play a for more important role. Stories and arguments animate our thinking and they often depend on the questions we have asked and the data we claim to use in developing our answers.

In many ways, I see teaching history as a cycle of inquiry: telling stories and building knowledge, establishing and clarifying questions, gathering and exploring additional evidence, and trying to produce and adjust answers and alternative narratives. We can do that over the course of one lesson, a small sequence of lessons, an entire topic, a major project, and even an entire course or year level.

At the heart of many chapters that follow in this book lies the idea that history is not simply the learning of facts (though that is crucial); it is the exploration of questions, evidence and proposed answers. If we place this at the centre of teaching history, we are less likely to see the subject collapse into atomised lessons, bits of information that do not seem connected, or the filling out of endless templates that feel like they go nowhere. We have, to put it more positively, a better chance of seeing history as a lively, interesting and meaningful subject with direction, purpose and relevance.

Managing the holistic process of inquiry

How the process of inquiry is managed in your class is, to a large degree, up to you. You might decide to guide students' learning in this process more tightly by setting the question you all explore together, providing a curated set of material for the students to develop their knowledge, and setting clearly defined tasks for them to complete to demonstrate and refine their learning.

Alternatively, you could open up this process and require the students to create questions they want to explore, find the sources to respond to the question, and then present their answers in a more creative manner.

In my experience, it is very rare for history teachers to simply leave students to "discover things for themselves" without any direction or structure as the defining approach to teaching the subject. In reality, most history teachers begin by establishing the main parameters of an inquiry; they set the guiding question(s), mandate the resources to explore, and state exactly how students will be expected to respond. Once the students' knowledge and confidence have grown, they are then likely to look for opportunities to open this process up to greater student choice – this is the bread and butter of my own teaching, for example. Even when students are given more freedom, most history teachers tend to guide this process quite carefully and remain actively involved by ensuring that students' questions and ideas make sense and have the potential for safe and meaningful learning, by checking in on student progress as they work, and also by providing feedback that assists them to refine their thinking and communication.

We might think of teaching history as a process of inquiry, then – as a kind of continuum, in which all aspects are more strictly controlled by the teacher at one end, moving towards, not random discovery, but guided independence at the other. Of course, there could also be, and often is, a blend of these approaches depending on the circumstances. One basic outline of this is provided in Table 4.2.

TABLE 4.2: Key aspects of historical inquiry mapped broadly to how independent students might be in the process (adapted from Gibson and Miles)[26]

	Established	Guided negotiation	Guided independence
Questions	Key question(s) for inquiry set and monitored by the teacher.	Teacher may present some established questions for inquiry and students collaborate and/or select.	Questions more collaboratively or independently generated with the teacher helping to check and refine.
Finding and analysing meaningful data	Central resources for exploring the question curated by the teacher.	Central resources synthesised from a mix of teacher curation and student collaboration and independent work such as research.	Students work more independently through research to find and synthesise sources with the teacher as point of active reference.

---

26 Lindsay Gibson and James Miles, "Inquiry Doesn't Just Happen" in Case, R., and Clark, P. (eds.) *Learning to Inquire in History, Geography and Social Studies: An Anthology for Secondary Teachers (4th Ed.)*, The Critical Thinking Consortium, 2020, p. 156.

	Established	Guided negotiation	Guided independence
Communicating, sharing and challenging stories and arguments	Parameters of communicating insights from inquiry defined by the teacher.	Parameters for communication established by the teacher but with some built-in options.	Students propose and then select appropriate forms in which to communicate ideas with input from the teacher.

Gradual release of responsibility

As a basic starting point, I would argue that a general gradual release of responsibility (GRR) approach is broadly useful for teaching secondary history, provided that it is used flexibly and not exclusively – it is always dangerous for pedagogical frameworks to become more important than the students or the subject(s) you teach.

GRR is an old idea and it is relatively straightforward. The model essentially advocates for a process in which learning is more tightly structured towards the beginning when students are new to a topic, skill or subject. As the students' knowledge and confidence grow, the teacher will give students greater freedom to work collaboratively and independently to practise, apply and shape aspects of the learning.[27] Importantly, the framework does not advocate for a process moving from 100 percent teacher to 100 percent student, rather that the roles of the teacher and student evolve over time as students' knowledge and confidence grow.

I have also found it helpful to avoid thinking of GRR as a singular and linear approach to secondary history. Instead, I tend to conceive of it as dynamically working across different scales of my teaching as I work with a class. Some examples of how I might use GRR at macro and micro levels of teaching and planning are outlined in Table 4.3 overleaf. These might be thought of as scales that, in reality, cascade into one another to form a dynamic, flexible and responsive process.

---

27 Douglas Fisher and Nancy Frey, *Better Learning Through Structured Teaching: A Framework for the Gradual Release of Responsibility*, ASCD, 2021.

TABLE 4.3: Using a basic gradual release of responsibility approach in secondary history

Across a course	When I begin a new course in which I will teach the same students for 6–12 months and cover multiple topics, I generally plan to release more cumulative responsibility to students over time. In earlier topics, I tend to teach in more structured ways (though still using GRR as outlined in the rows below) and aim to open this up to varying degrees as the students become more familiar with my expectations, and more confident with the central substantive, disciplinary and practical knowledge. In some cases, I aim to give the students considerable freedom over time by moving towards what I have called "guided independence" in Table 4.2.
Across a unit	Generally, I also hope to give students more room for independence over the course of each topic. I usually try to begin by establishing the key learning aims and goals for the topic, setting the pace and ensuring that students understand what standards of knowledge and work are expected. In many scenarios, it may be a few weeks before I give the students major independence (though they would already be consistently doing independent work within the lessons). By doing this, I have used the first weeks of a topic to clearly establish good routines, set high expectations, and model and formatively assess key ideas and skills before letting the students work more independently through selecting issues or themes to research and/or apply their knowledge and skills more broadly.
Sequence of lessons	Within larger units, I also often use a GRR approach when I want to teach a specific skill such as developing written responses incorporating primary source material. I might, for example, set aside 3–4 lessons in which I: • begin by explaining the key conventions of that mode of writing • examine and discuss strong written samples with the class (usually a mix of whole-class, small-group and individual work) • explain and model key processes that help to generate quality writing • require students to practise aspects of the writing independently • provide feedback on their work so that it can be refined and improved.
Individual lessons	On an even smaller scale, I often also use the basic GRR approach when introducing new activities within a lesson. For example, I might be trying to teach students how to engage with wartime propaganda of the First World War. After introducing the aims and structure of the individual lesson, I might then demonstrate to students some of the key questions I often ask when confronted with new sources of propaganda using a sample source. After that, we might explore a second example as a class, with me asking lots of questions and clarifying key ideas before letting students explore other examples in small groups or individually before sharing their work with the class.

Many people use the old expression "I do, we do, you do" when referring to a model such as GRR. Though this may be applicable in some subjects, I find it quite limited in secondary history, particularly if it is treated as a rigidly linear process (I do, *then* we do, *then* you do). Primarily, this is because not all meaningful activities in history require this kind of procedural approach. For example, a teacher might be aiming to work in depth with a small collection of primary sources with their students before getting them to do some extended writing. Before they begin examining the sources, students would need to develop some substantive knowledge so that the primary sources can be contextualised. Building this crucial substantive knowledge could be done through watching a short documentary, conducting some independent reading from a textbook, and some whole-class discussion. None of this really requires modelling or a structured "I do, we do, you do" approach. It is a good reminder that catchy little phrases in education, however useful, rarely capture the complexity of what quality teaching really is across all subjects.

Chapter summary

- History is best understood as a holistic process that involves many key components: exploring narratives, asking questions, developing factual knowledge, communicating ideas, revising ideas and more.
- The notion of inquiry in history here refers more to the kinds of thinking and intellectual work involved in the subject than a specific mode of pedagogy.
- Using gradual release of responsibility can be a powerful approach to teaching and learning history in many contexts, particularly when students have less knowledge and confidence.
- The aim of teaching should be to increase students' ability to work more independently over time.

End of chapter questions

Questions for reflection and discussion	Questions to ask experienced teachers
1. How would you explain the concept of "historical inquiry"? 2. What are the benefits of treating history as a holistic process? 3. Re-examine Table 4.2. How might the approaches set out in the columns be mixed together over the course of a topic? 4. Explain how gradual release of responsibility can be used to help structure learning so that students develop into more confident and independent learners.	1. How do you manage student autonomy in the different year levels that you teach? 2. How do you help less-confident students in history classes?

Further reading

Resource	Why bother reading it?
Arthur Chapman, "Historical Interpretation as the Foundational Concept for History Education", *Revista de Historia (Concepción)*, Vol. 31, 2024, pp. 1–25	In this article, Arthur Chapman argues that the concept of "historical interpretations" lies at the foundation of history education. Instead of viewing historical concepts and skills as distinct, this argument suggests that they form part of a larger coherent whole.
Janet van Drie and Carla von Boxtel, "Historical Reasoning: Towards a Framework for Analyzing Students' Reasoning about the Past", *Education Psychology Review*, Vol. 20, No. 2, 2008, pp. 87–110	This article provides a synthesis of ideas relating to historical thinking to make a case for working with students to develop their historical reasoning.
Bob Bain, Arthur Chapman, Alison Kitson and Tamara Schreirer (eds.), *History Education and Historical Enquiry*, Information Age Publishing, 2023	This book includes a range of chapters that discuss key aspects of historical inquiry. Across the book, the chapters cover a useful range of theoretical and practical ideas that draw together key insights into the teaching of history as a process of inquiry.

Resource	Why bother reading it?
Douglas Fisher and Nancy Frey, *Better Learning Through Structured Teaching: A Framework for the Gradual Release of Responsibility*, ASCD, 2021	This is a well-known distillation of the gradual release of responsibility framework. It is clearly set out and easy to read, but it is not subject-specific, so there are a lot of examples provided that are irrelevant to history and it is important to keep a critical eye on some of the suggestions made in parts. Though it is worth being familiar with the book, it is not a direct guide for using GRR in secondary history, so I would not try to use it as a specific model for teaching the subject.

CHAPTER 5

Adapt the discipline for schools

We often hear that history is a discipline and that we are introducing students to this through school subjects. I am convinced that this is a helpful way of thinking, provided that we treat it cautiously and intelligently.

Most importantly, I would argue that we need to be careful that we do not assume that this means that all students must be treated as mini-historians, or be required to act like them, all the time. Many students do not want to be historians and a large number will, in fact, never study history any further than required in their schooling. Expecting these students to assume the identity of historians could be as confusing as assuming that they must consider themselves "chefs" because they also took your colleague's cooking class. Of course, some students might go on to be historians and we should celebrate that, but this is rare. To be clear, I am not suggesting that our students *cannot* be historians, but assuming that they all are by virtue of their enrolment in your class might be counterproductive.

Paul Kirschner also makes a further warning about working with academic disciplines in school contexts. He suggests, helpfully in my view, that sometimes we can assume that the "epistemology" of a discipline – the way the professionals do their work and build new knowledge – should always be the "pedagogy" we employ in schools.[28] To put this simply, he is suggesting that we might make the mistake of assuming that if we see historians doing it, we should get our school's students in history to do it in the same manner. The danger is that there is a more complex situation in play.[29]

Kirschner makes a strong case, for example, that this can be dangerous because professionals carry with them enormous knowledge and experience that our students in secondary schools could almost never possess. With less

---

[28] Kirschner, P. A. "Epistemology or pedagogy, that is the question" in Tobias, S., and Duffy, T. M., (eds.) *Constructivist Instruction: Success or Failure?*, Routledge, 2009, pp. 144–57.

[29] This is a similar argument to that developed by Daniel Willingham in *Why Don't Students Like School? (2nd Ed.)*, Jossey-Bass, 2021, pp. 143–65.

experience in the subject, we cannot assume that all students immediately have the knowledge, subject-wisdom and confidence to perform to the full depth or repertoire of a professor with 30 years' experience in the field. This sets up an important opportunity to consider how we might intelligently and selectively adapt and translate the academic discipline of history for secondary classrooms. In fact, this consideration has been a consistent theme of history education research for decades.[30]

Working towards historical confidence

Rather than consider our work as history teachers to be training mini-historians, I would argue that a more productive aim, apart from trying to communicate the fascination and joy of exploring the past, is to build students' historical discernment, confidence and agility. What I mean by that is their ability to remember important ideas about the past, their ability to think about the past in complex ways, and also their ability to be flexible with history by engaging with it through books, film, virtual resources, museums and more. The more I can help students develop this confidence and agility, the more successful I generally feel.

Concretely, I would hope that if I had students in my class over the course of several years, they would have a well-rounded understanding of key topics and eras we have explored. Additionally, I would hope that they would recognise and be able to begin to explain with specific examples why history is complex and contestable. I would also hope that they could appreciate how history operates across different spaces and genres such as books, films and museums and in their own lives. Ultimately, this would hopefully enable them to develop their own ideas about history that are informed and insightful.

Some students will develop this confidence and agility to a mature degree that could be genuinely intimidating. Others will grow in their confidence but may not get nearly as far. That is perfectly acceptable and expected. The question is: have I helped the students move forward (preferably while still enjoying the subject)?

---

30 See, for example, the discussion about research into the use of historical source material provided by Abby Reisman and Sarah McGrew in "Reading in History Education: Text, Sources and Evidence", in Metzger, S., and Harris, L. (eds.) *The Wiley International Handbook of History Teaching and Learning*, John Wiley and Sons, 2018, pp. 529-50.

In schools, I would argue that we work towards this confidence and agility by focusing on three overlapping areas of knowledge.[31] These are outlined in Table 5.1.

TABLE 5.1: Substantive, disciplinary and practical knowledge (which are best thought of as overlapping rather than entirely discrete forms of knowledge in history)

Substantive knowledge	Substantive knowledge might be thought of as the factual basis of the question, issue or topic we are exploring. This is the meaningful data we need to begin to give shape to the past. It includes narratives, basic factual information, key terms and concepts (such as empire, revolution, democracy and class), individuals and groups and more. It is important to remember that "substantive knowledge" is more than just isolated "facts".
Disciplinary knowledge	This is useful knowledge developed through insights from the discipline. We might include here things like knowledge of causation, since historians argue a lot about that. It might also include change and continuity, the role of historical evidence in shaping arguments and interpretations, perspectives and more.
Practical knowledge	Practical knowledge allows us to perform important tasks in history – for example, developing a narrative, structuring an argument in essay form, using an academic database for research, producing writing that draws on a mix of the student's knowledge and some given source material, and delivering a coherent oral argument.

These three areas of knowledge should interlock regularly as you explore topics with students, allowing them to deepen their understanding in each area and make incremental growth in their historical confidence and agility.

---

31 Here I agree with Michael Fordham's argument that, although considering types of knowledge in history can be useful, an overly strict distinction between them can be counter-productive. See "Types of Knowledge in a History Curriculum", *Clio et cetera* (Blog), 20 March 2017: https://clioetcetera.com/2017/03/20/types-of-knowledge-in-a-history-curriculum/

DIAGRAM 5.1: Adapting the history discipline for schools

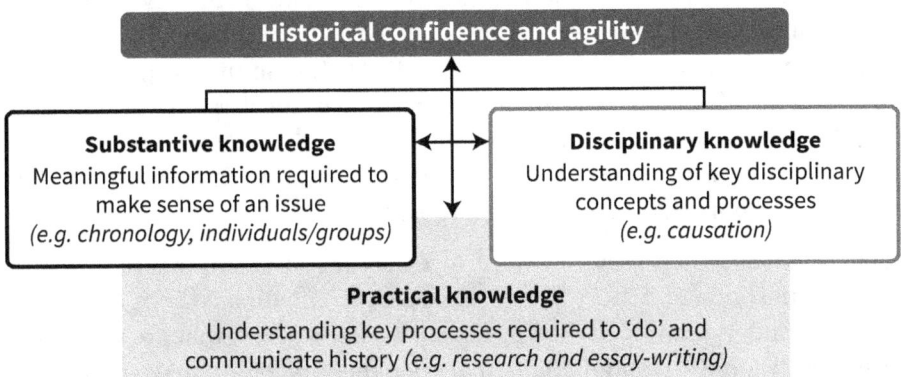

Substantive knowledge

It is difficult to engage intelligently with the past if you know little about it. Whether you are writing, speaking or making films about the past, the more you know, the more refined your ideas and approach can be.

To teach history effectively you will be well served if you develop a strong knowledge of the topics that you teach (see Chapter 6). You will also need to ensure that as you teach the students, you help them build crucial knowledge too. There is no other way forward; otherwise history is likely to become little more than a shallow and opinionated exchange of ideas. The more useful knowledge you possess and can adapt helpfully for your secondary students, and the more useful knowledge your students possess, the more likely it is that your classes will be able to do analytical work insightfully. If you want students to become more critical and creative historical thinkers, they need to acquire factual knowledge in the process of exploring the past.[32]

Opinionated assertion or insightful argument?

Imagine a secondary school student who enjoys debating aspects of history. This student thrives on the big questions: Who was the most effective Roman emperor? Why did Europe become a dominant global force in the industrial age? Could the Russian empire have avoided collapse in 1917? Was Hitler or Stalin the more powerful dictator? Why did Australia develop into a multicultural nation? It is not hard to imagine this student offering confident

---

32 Daniel Willingham, *Why Don't Students Like School? (2nd Ed.)*, Jossey-Bass, 2021, pp. 25–56.

answers to these questions with a shallow depth of knowledge about any of them – this kind of thing happens regularly and not just in history classrooms. Their opinions can probably be quickly and easily challenged by pointing out major gaps or errors in their knowledge. The ability to offer opinions about questions of history is no guarantee that those answers are insightful or that they are based on accurate, intelligent or the most useful information. Engaging with history intelligently involves much more than the confidence to assert an opinion, though that is part of it.

While we would certainly not want to discourage this student's interest in the big questions of history, we would want to encourage them to develop a deeper understanding of the key facts, ideas and issues that are relevant to answering them. This should help to deepen their ideas and make them more convincing.

There is an important caveat here. Teaching history is not simply an exercise in amassing information (for the teacher or the student) such that one might dominate a world-class history quiz. It is no good expecting your students to learn and remember detailed or esoteric information about a period you are studying together if this is disconnected, arbitrary or unused. Knowledge is crucial, but it must be thought of strategically and intentionally, and not every fact that is taught across a sequence of lessons needs to be remembered forever.[33]

Substantive knowledge: working with students

Within each specific topic you teach, it is important to begin thinking about what students at their current stage of schooling need to know. Here a curriculum document such as a syllabus will provide some guidance, but it will not be exhaustive. The assessment tasks and other major activities students are working towards should also help frame this knowledge, and experience teaching the topic a few times will also help.

At a minimum, you should be planning to include regular activities in your lessons that help the students build and retain meaningful knowledge for the topics you explore. This could mean some substantial reading (appropriate for their age and ability), viewing a documentary and taking notes, working through a small collection of primary documents thoroughly, creating or

---

[33] For example, see Jonathan Grande, "Why I teach pupils things I don't need them to remember forever: The role of takeaways in shaping a history curriculum", *Teaching History*, Vol. 192, 2023, pp. 18-29.

adapting a timeline to ensure that they understand the overarching narrative, independently researching an individual, group or theme, and defining important terms that will allow them to use language more accurately. It could also mean something much more creative.

It would then involve regularly revisiting that material to ensure that the students know it and can use it in meaningful ways (see Chapter 23). It may be of no use if a student can remember a set of isolated facts about history but cannot connect them with other facts, use them to point out patterns, make sense of them with broader concepts, use them to shape a narrative, use them to develop comparisons with another aspect of the topic, and so on.

Although factual knowledge is sometimes seen as the less interesting component of history – compared with making arguments and the like – I would disagree. Factual information can be very stimulating for students when they know little about a topic. For example, I often begin new topics with some brief factual information to try to capture the students' interest. When exploring the inter-war crisis with older students, for example, I often show a specific political map comparing Europe in 1914 and 1939 and point out that there were 17 dictatorial regimes in power by the end of the 1930s. That one fact – 17 dictatorships – is often shocking and opens up a range of questions that we can then begin to explore, such as: Why were there so many dictatorships in this period? Were they all similar? One fact and a map to convey a big story have become the launchpad for interesting discussions that lead directly to bigger questions and more analytical and creative work. We would, I therefore suggest, be unwise to underestimate the power of factual knowledge in the larger processes of teaching secondary history.

Disciplinary knowledge

Anyone who has studied history seriously at secondary school or university should be aware that historical knowledge is contested.[34] At the very least this means being aware that the narratives and interpretations historians develop often differ and that sometimes they even dispute basic facts about the past. One reason for this is that historians operate in different ways using different assumptions, theories, sources and methods.[35]

Many professional historians do, however, share important similarities in the way they work. Most, for example, attempt to develop narratives and

---

34 Daniel Woolf, *A Global History of History*, Cambridge University Press, 2011.
35 For some abbreviated examples of this, see Jonathon Dallimore, *Contesting the Great War: An Introduction to Key Debates of the First World War*, History Teachers' Association of New South Wales, 2017.

arguments about the past based on dependable evidence – they do not consciously try to invent characters or events as an author of fiction might. Most historians also argue about underlying themes such as causation (why did the First World War break out?) or change and continuity (how much did life in Australia really change after Federation in 1901?). They also often argue about evidence, particularly when new documents or artefacts are discovered.

While we should not expect most students in secondary school to begin immediately mimicking all the complex procedures of professional historians, there is no reason why they cannot be introduced to some of the ways in which historians think and work at a level appropriate for their age and context. Students can, for example, be introduced to the ways in which historians might engage with documentary or photographic evidence or the kinds of arguments historians might make about the causes of a particular event.[36] Not only is this possible, but many students are likely to be interested in these aspects of history if they are introduced thoughtfully and appropriately.

Over the past 50 years, teachers and scholars in many parts of the world have attempted to conduct research into these disciplinary elements of "doing history". In England, for example, the Schools History Project launched in 1972 attempted to make school history livelier, in part, by providing students with more opportunities to explore primary sources and engage with the past in a more critical manner.[37] Over time, this evolved into research around what many people call "historical thinking", which explores the ways in which secondary history teachers might adapt and model the best approaches to history used by academic historians in their scholarship.

What is historical thinking?

The expression "historical thinking" generally refers to the ways in which historians think about, process and analyse the past. There are many different models attempting to capture some of these cognitive processes but there is also overlap among many. It is common, for example, to identify a range of important concepts and skills that regularly feature in historians' work. These include those outlined in Table 5.2, but it is important to recognise that these themes are not exhaustive.

---

[36] See Sam Wineburg, *Historical Thinking and Other Unnatural Acts: Charting the Future of Teaching the Past*, Temple University Press, 2001, and Peter Seixas and John Morton, *The Big Six Historical Thinking Concepts*, Nelson, 2012.

[37] The Schools History Project is still active in the United Kingdom. See: https://www.schoolshistoryproject.co.uk/about/

TABLE 5.2: Common dimensions of historical thinking

Significance	This refers to the way historians argue about the relative importance of events, individuals, artefacts, sites and more. Many societies, such as Australia, for example, have statues and monuments to the First and Second World Wars, but fewer to other events, suggesting that, culturally, we see some events as more important to remember than others. Why? Is this reasonable? What is forgotten in this process?
Causation	Historians often argue about why things in the past happened. Some might stress economic forces at work, others stress the role of key individuals or groups, while others argue that culture might play a larger role. Often, historians are not attempting to make a case that history is driven by a single factor, but they do often emphasise one or some over others, and this leads to debate.
Change and Continuity	Another common dimension of historical debate is contesting the nature of change and continuity. Did, for example, the Russian Revolution lead to fundamental change, or was it more a process of reforming Russia along traditional authoritarian lines? Did the Russian Revolution simply replace "tsars" with "commissars" as is sometimes said, and, more fundamentally, did the continuities ultimately outweigh the changes?
Perspectives	How and why do people view the past from such varied perspectives? How do these contribute to our understanding of the past? Whose perspectives should be foregrounded in an exploration of the past?
Sources and evidence	What kinds of sources are helpful in exploring the past? How do we get useful evidence out of this material? What can we really and confidently know about the past on the basis of this material? What do we do when there are significant gaps in the source material?
Interpretations	How and why do people arrive at such varied interpretations of the past? How do different interpretations help us make sense of the past? Are some interpretations better than others? If so, why?

Many school history curriculum documents now include some explicit reference to these disciplinary aspects. This is certainly true of many Australian states, but it has also become common in countries such as Canada, Singapore, Britain, the United States and the Republic of Korea.

While this academic research into historical thinking and similar ideas can be complex, it has a reasonably simple aim at its core: to find useable ways of adapting the work of historians for school students. Many researchers, such as Carla Peck, Peter Seixas, Sam Wineburg, Christine Counsell, Stéphane Lévesque, Arthur Chapman and Lindsay Gibson, would argue that this has the potential to help students even if they are not planning on engaging formally with history beyond school – and I agree. For a start, they would argue that disciplinary aspects of history can equip students with ways of thinking that can help them navigate historical representations in the wider world. This includes thinking critically about the narratives they are confronted with in public life on a regular basis.[38] It should be noted, however, that this disciplinary approach to secondary history is certainly not without its critics.[39]

Disciplinary knowledge: working with students

The disciplinary aspects of history can be some of the most challenging to teach in secondary schools. They can be complex and difficult, and they often require exposure and practice over extended periods. It takes time to gain confidence working with different kinds of historical sources, for example. In addition, it is true that if disciplinary aspects of history are overemphasised too early in some contexts, it can turn students off the subject, and that is clearly counterproductive.

Nevertheless, decades of teaching history in many countries has confirmed that students of many different backgrounds and abilities can begin to work with disciplinary aspects of history and enjoy it. Though their work might express imprecision and naïve claims about the past compared with a professor at a high-profile university, you might also be pleasantly surprised at what many students can achieve when they are taught effectively.

Increasing the complexity of the game

When I was in primary school, I began to play soccer – football if you prefer – with my local team. In my first couple of years, at training and on the field, we were not required to learn all the rules that professional players

---

38 See for example: Stéphane Lévesque and Arthur Chapman, "Ukraine Invasion: How History Can Empower People to Make Sense of Russia's War", *The Conversation*, 9 May 2022: https://theconversation.com/ukraine-invasion-how-history-can-empower-people-to-make-sense-of-russias-war-181999

39 For a summary of some of these criticisms, see Lindsay Gibson, "What Is Historical Thinking? Part III: Critiques of Historical Thinking", *Canadian Historical Association*: https://cha-shc.ca/teachers-learning-bl/what-is-historical-thinking-part-iii/

in major leagues have to adhere to. We were first introduced to scoring, field dimensions, and fundamental rules such as not touching the ball with your hands unless you were the goalkeeper. As we grew, the local league I played in then introduced more complex rules such as offside, and our coaches began to emphasise the unique roles of the positions we were to play on the field. As we got even older, we began to design and implement strategic "plays" on the field, depending on the team we faced off against. We were playing the same essential game all along, but we were learning to play it in more complex and interesting ways as our knowledge and confidence increased.

Although playing soccer is obviously not identical to learning history, the basic approach here is sensible. Begin by introducing novices to the fundamentals and then increase the complexity as they become more competent, but make sure they have a bit of fun in the process too. Any decent history curriculum document will include this general idea by design. Students in senior years will be required to demonstrate a more complex understanding of history than students in Year 7, but they are all still "playing the same game".

Perhaps the most important factor to keep in mind when introducing secondary students to the disciplinary aspects of history, then, is that it needs to be done strategically and carefully. In many circumstances, this would be done once students have already begun to learn some of the substantive knowledge central to the topic or question in focus and by explaining and modelling the disciplinary ideas you plan to foreground.

In the earlier years of secondary school, this is likely to involve an introduction to basic ideas such as the nature of chronology, the role of sources in developing ideas about the past, and some key concepts such as causation. As students progress into the later years of secondary school, it might involve engaging more deeply with historical debates and doing more sustained work with primary sources, scholarly interpretations, popular representations of the past in films or museums, and more extensive independent research.

Appreciating the various ways of doing history is also important since many students will engage with these once they leave school. Many will travel internationally and visit historic sites, and many will watch historical films. They will be confronted with stories about the past claiming to justify all kinds of political decisions that they may need to respond to through voting and other civic activity. Some familiarity with the fact that history can be constructed in various mediums and that it is wise to thoughtfully consume them is both individually and collectively useful. Helping students understand and appreciate this can be a powerful aspect of teaching history.

Across the years of secondary school, it can be useful to conduct historical film studies with students. It can also be useful to take groups to museums and help them understand how these institutions operate. It can be helpful to look at political uses of the past and discuss how they might be thoughtfully responded to.

Importantly too, most students need to be shown how to do all of this. If historical thinking really is an "unnatural act", then most students cannot be expected to just be able to do it.[40] At 14 years of age, I was certainly not ready to be given a collection of complex documents with an expectation that I would be able to independently produce insightful stories or comments about the past that might have stood up to reasonable scrutiny – I needed to be shown the tricks of the trade, many times. So, part of what it means to teach students to work in disciplinary ways is modelling, scaffolding and demonstration, so that they develop their confidence and become more independent over time.

Practical knowledge

Making progress in secondary history also requires a considerable amount of practical knowledge. We might think of practical knowledge in this context as any technical know-how the students require to complete meaningful tasks such as using research databases, composing meaningful written work, and so on. Most obviously when we think of history, for example, we might think of writing an essay, which is a technical process. It requires specific knowledge of how introductions, paragraphs, evidence and conclusions work at a bare minimum. It also requires the use of unique substantive and disciplinary knowledge, meaning that history essays are emphatically *not* identical to essays in other subjects.

Diagram 5.1 points out a crucial issue regarding practical knowledge in secondary history: it must be grounded in the unique substantive and disciplinary knowledge that students develop. As many students quickly realise, a strong history essay is quite different to a strong essay in English literature, even though both might share some general features such as an overall structure including an introduction, body and conclusion. Strong history essays respond to different kinds of questions, make use of different kinds of evidence, make different kinds of analytical claims, and more. In other words, practical knowledge combines technical processes such as writing and essay-construction with the substantive and disciplinary knowledge of

---

[40] Sam Wineburg, *Historical Thinking and Other Unnatural Acts: Charting the Future of Teaching the Past*, Temple University Press, 2001.

the subject and, collectively, this produces the unique emphasis of history as a subject in schools.

The kinds of practical knowledge that students require in history might vary depending on the topic, but there are some common features across the course of secondary schooling. In most jurisdictions, history students need to be able to write in extended form (at least in their senior years), they need to be able to handle various kinds of source material, and they are often required to present historical arguments in verbal and written form. In addition to this, students might also be required to present ideas in more creative ways, including producing podcasts, museum displays or videos. Though less common, these forms of communication also require the students to develop unique practical knowledge.

It is important that, as soon as possible, you begin to look at strong samples of a range of student work to see this practical knowledge in action. Your appreciation of what students can do in terms of writing, speaking and other forms of communication will only grow by looking at a wide range of samples, and this will, in turn, contribute to your ability to help students make progress in these practical areas of their work. If your faculty or jurisdiction has sample history essays, for example, a good place to start is closely examining a range of responses reflecting upper, middle and lower quality to see what students can do in that age range.

Practical knowledge: working with students

Most students will need clear guidance when it comes to technical aspects of practical knowledge. In fact, a key principle to remember when requiring students to present their ideas in any form is that they will usually need to explore what the genre's typical conventions are, what separates stronger work from that of poorer quality, and how one might begin to perform intelligently in that genre. This is true of writing essays, producing podcasts, and delivering oral presentations. All mediums of communication and performance require knowledge of conventions, quality and process, and students may not already possess this knowledge, so part of the common teaching cycle would be to explore these aspects directly and explicitly.

Writing an imaginary diary entry

When I was in secondary school, I remember being required to "imagine I was a figure" from the particular period of history we were studying, so that we could then write an imaginary diary entry from that individual's perspective describing their daily life – this actually happened several times when I was in my younger years at school. I recall enjoying the imaginary process of this task, but I also remember finding it quite difficult. This was not because I did not know enough about the period, but because I had never kept a diary and I was completely unfamiliar with what people would normally write in them. Unless the teacher explained what diaries are for, how they tend to be written and so on – and they did this sometimes – how could I write a high-quality diary entry? If I were not shown these dimensions of the work, I would be guessing at what a good diary entry might look like, and that is a recipe for honest mistakes. What this story reminds us of is the importance of making conventions, expectations of quality, and processes clear for students when we require them to communicate in technical forms. This is true if the medium is writing, podcasting, speaking or something else entirely.

In most topics that you teach, a limited number of practical tasks should be foregrounded. For example, in one topic, the students might work towards writing an essay, and this would then become the central feature of their practical knowledge for that topic. In another topic, students might be working closely with a range of historical sources, and their ability to communicate with and about sources would then become the central feature of their practical knowledge.

Perhaps the most important point about practical knowledge is that it needs to be developed incrementally and with an aim to increasing the students' confidence through modelling, practice and feedback. As Rob Marzano suggests: "Effective practice transforms procedural knowledge that must be laboriously executed to procedural knowledge that is executed fluently".[41]

Chapter summary

- Because secondary students are not trained professional historians, it is best to adapt the discipline for school contexts and aim to build students towards historical confidence and agility.
- There are three overlapping types of knowledge central to secondary history: substantive, disciplinary and practical.
- Teachers need to be prepared to balance all three if students are to develop their confidence in this subject.

---

41 Robert Marzano, *Art and Science of Teaching: A Comprehensive Framework for Effective Instruction*, Association of Supervision and Curriculum Development, 2007, p. 79.

End of chapter questions

Questions for reflection and discussion	Questions to ask experienced teachers
1. Why might it be difficult to treat history in secondary schools as identical to history in the academy? 2. What are the differences between substantive, disciplinary and practical knowledge as set out in this chapter? How might they overlap in teaching history?	1. What are the hardest aspects of history to teach to secondary students? 2. What kinds of mediums do you require students to communicate in most in history? Writing, speaking, digital, other? How do you help them develop their confidence?

Further reading

Resource	Why bother reading it?
Christine Counsell, "The Fertility of Substantive Knowledge: In Search of Its Hidden, Generative Power" in Ian Davies (ed.) *Debates in History Teaching (2nd Ed.)*, London: Routledge, pp. 80–99	Counsell's chapter explores how substantive knowledge can unlock powerful learning opportunities for students such that it should always be taken seriously.
Stéphane Lévesque, *Thinking Historically: Educating Students for the 21st Century*, University of Toronto Press, 2009	Lévesque's book offers a broad overview of historical thinking with excellent practical tips too. This will help you understand some of the key ways students might learn to "do history".
Carol Betram, "Exploring the Concept of a 'Historical Gaze'", *Yesterday&Today*, No. 3, 2008, pp. 1–9	This article outlines an interesting and useful perspective considering what makes historical ideas unique compared with other school subjects.
Michael Stephen Schiro, *Curriculum Theory: Conflicting Visions and Enduring Concerns (2nd Ed.)*, Sage, 2013	Chapter 1 provides a readable introduction to several broad approaches to curriculum that help locate the "disciplinary" approach to school subjects among other prominent alternatives. Chapter 2 provides further detail on the "scholar academic ideology" that shares some similarities with the arguments in this book.

CHAPTER 6

Nurture your curriculum confidence

Aspects of teaching secondary history can be highly creative. Planning topic sequences, putting together a resource for students from primary sources, and designing rich and interesting projects that your students enjoy are all common ways that history teachers embrace this creativity. Designing lessons is also widely reported to be an aspect of teaching that many professionals enjoy and consider to be important.[42]

The opportunity to be creative and the genuine fulfilment this can bring can also mask some potential dangers. It can take considerable time to find, edit and curate primary sources, for example, particularly for topics or themes that you are not familiar with. When you are less experienced, piecing together boutique sequences of lessons can also be difficult. This kind of work can also encourage a misleading impression that unique resources created by a teacher *must* always be better or that they *must* lead to more meaningful learning than resources that are given, borrowed or found.

Much public time and energy has been spent on arguing about teacher resources and, in some jurisdictions, enormous amounts of public money have been spent on producing curriculum material in the hope that this would magically reduce teacher workloads. Beginning teachers too often make the mistake of believing that if they had access to pre-planned units of work, their planning time would be essentially eliminated and the path to high-quality lessons made swift and easy.

I am sceptical of this even though I see the value in having some curriculum resources available – they are already accessible through textbooks, cultural

---

42 See, for example, Mihajla Gavin and Meghan Stacey, "Tackle Teachers' Workloads but Leave Lesson Planning to the Experts", *Sydney Morning Herald*, 3 February 2024: https://www.smh.com.au/business/workplace/tackle-teachers-workloads-but-leave-lesson-planning-to-the-experts-20240201-p5f1oi.html

institutions, documentaries, free websites and communally shared material. My concern is that using quality history resources that you have not created can still be time-consuming and that false promises of radical reductions in planning time can further disappoint. If you are using some curated sources, for example, it still means reading the texts carefully, checking the activities provided, considering adaptations that might be required for your class, and then perhaps deciding not to use the material anyway because it might be too simple or complex for the students you are working with – that does not mean it is of poor quality, only that it is not well suited to your circumstances. In short, ready-made resources still take time to explore, adapt and use and, in some cases, turn out to be of poorer quality than one might have hoped.

I would argue that, instead of thinking primarily about resources as the key path to efficient teaching, we should keep our main sights trained on developing our curriculum confidence. Over the longer term, this will ultimately be a more powerful predictor of efficiency and quality and it will be this that gives you the most power to quickly borrow, adapt or create high-quality material. Additionally, some research suggests that students respond more positively to teachers who possess the expertise to remain flexible than to those who rigidly and unimaginatively follow curriculum plans.[43]

What is curriculum confidence?

I use the expression curriculum confidence to refer to a history teacher's level of clarity, efficiency and independence regarding the curriculum they teach. Those with less curriculum confidence need more assistance in implementing a curriculum, and those with more confidence can operate with a higher degree of efficiency and freedom. The latter teachers understand what the curriculum requires, can see various possibilities in meeting those requirements, and can quickly plan quality ways of addressing them.

If you have already begun to work in schools, hopefully you have met several teachers who seem secure when teaching the curriculum for their subject area. They teach lessons consistently well, regularly use effective resources, manage classroom behaviour with composure, set clear and useful assessment tasks for the subject and, when asked about what they are doing, can rationalise in some depth and with clarity the choices they have made regarding topics, lessons, resources and assessment. These teachers may even have thoughtful ideas about the direction of the curriculum and how it might be improved.

---

43 Pedro de Bruyckere, Paul Kirschner and Yvonne Xian-han Huang, "Authentic Teachers: Student Criteria Perceiving the Authenticity of Teachers", *Cogent Education*, Vol. 3, No. 1, 2016, pp. 1–15.

These individuals are likely to be genuine subject experts with a high degree of curriculum confidence. Where it might take a less confident teacher 10-15 minutes to evaluate a potential resource for a lesson, it might take these individuals two. They can draw on their confidence to make faster and better decisions, which can cut down planning time and free them up to concentrate on other matters.

Like most aspects of teaching, curriculum confidence takes time to develop, and there are few shortcuts. It emerges from a rich combination of teaching experience and reflecting on that teaching through reading, discussion, observation and feedback. This confidence may develop accidentally, but it is best thought of as something worked on gradually and intentionally.

Starting out with lower curriculum confidence

The model outlined in Diagram 6.1 (below) offers a basic overview of some of the many aspects of teaching that you will be beginning to balance as you start teaching secondary history. You will be working in a community, and you will need to implement a given curriculum. Most specifically, this involves working with students to teach lessons and whole units of work, assess students and provide feedback, manage behaviour, and more. To do this, you will require resources and assessment activities for the topics you teach and you will need to draw upon the expertise of your community through the school, professional associations and other contexts.

DIAGRAM 6.1: Curriculum confidence

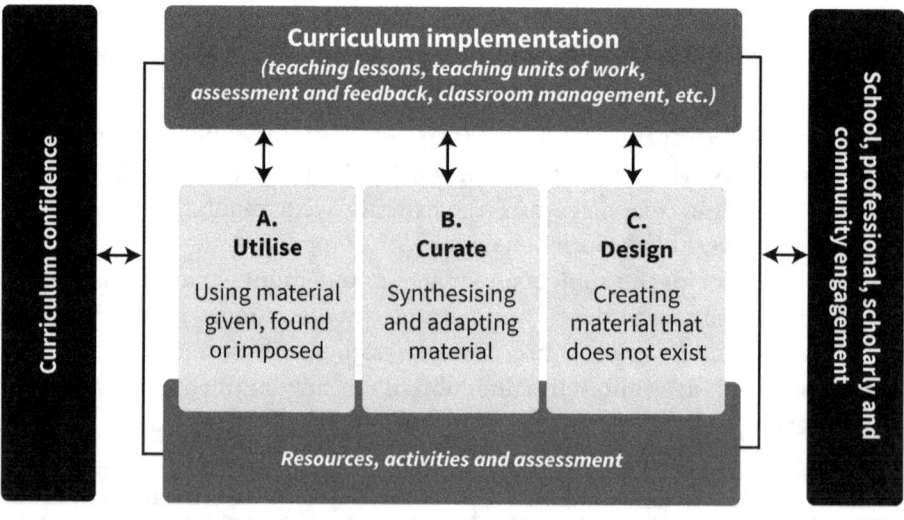

It would be rare for a beginning secondary history teacher to have no curriculum confidence whatsoever. If history is your main teaching area, you have studied some history at university and, perhaps not too long ago, in school. These experiences mean that you have at least a basic idea of what teaching and learning history might look like. Your work in your teaching degree and on practicum should then continue to build your curriculum confidence incrementally.

It is common, however, to feel overwhelmed as you begin teaching, so it makes sense to have a plan for how you might begin to operate when your curriculum confidence is lower.

In these earlier stages of your career, you will have to quickly learn the arts of triaging and prioritising, as these will serve you well over the course of your career. There are many aspects of teaching that you do not have any control over, such as your timetable and the requirement to teach your lessons, provide feedback on student work through assessment, write reports, and so on.

There are, however, aspects that you have more control over. Most obviously, when selecting and resourcing topics that you teach, you could try to heroically create all of the resources, activities and assessment tasks from the ground up, but you would quickly hit a wall, as you simply will not have time.

Instead, it is probably wise to rely more on what I have called in Diagram 6.1 utilisation and curation in the earlier stages of your career. This would involve using material such as teaching programs, resources and assessments that you did not create but that clearly and effectively address the learning requirements of your classes. To make this even more specific, I often tell beginning teachers that in an ideal world they should plan to rely on utilising and curating for about 85 percent of the resources and assessments they use across their units of work. As their curriculum confidence grows, they may choose to rely more on design as a way of replacing older material or that which has not worked as well as expected. The goal is not, however, to reach a point where you design all your resources and assessments. That would be unnecessary because, as your curriculum confidence grows, you are likely to be able to adapt existing resources quickly and turn them into high-quality learning.

Though it should go without saying, experience suggests that it has to be noted: if you use, borrow or adapt resources from a colleague, you *must* ensure that it is freely available to be used or that you have openly sought permission to use the material and acknowledge the creator wherever necessary and possible. Though many teachers are generous and happy to share, it is polite and professional to operate transparently and never try to pass off the work of someone else as your own. It is unethical and it is likely to catch up with you eventually.

Are boutique resources always better?

It is important to challenge the impression that quality resources for teaching history can *only* come in the form of boutique material made by the teacher and that they are always precisely fine-tuned for a highly specific group of students.

In fact, quality material for teaching history can come from many sources that already exist, including textbooks, documentaries, short films and animations, curated material from museums and cultural institutions, and resource banks created by faculties and colleagues. If these materials have been put together thoughtfully by experienced teachers and experts, it would be naïve to think that an individual teacher in the early stages of their career would be able to create better material on every subject or theme across a curriculum. So, in short, we should expect that many quality resources will already exist to be used and adapted thoughtfully by teachers.

That said, creating resources and assessments can be a powerful way of developing your curriculum confidence and it can be an enjoyable process. It can also be a way to express and refine your subject expertise.

Some brief thoughts on creating resources

Before deciding to commit to the creation of new material, it is generally worth considering a few questions to ensure that your time and effort are well-spent. These are outlined in Table 6.1.

TABLE 6.1: Some questions to consider before creating new resources

Is this aspect of the topic crucial for me to be spending significant time on, or is it more peripheral to the central themes and questions I want to explore?	If it is central, then any effort to create new material may be more justifiable. If it is a smaller aspect of a larger topic that you could easily address more quickly, then you may decide to use what is already available and adapt it the best way you can.
Am I sure that nothing else already exists that would fill in the gaps I have or improve my current collection of resources?	It is often worth double-checking that you have not missed another resource before committing to the work of creating something new. This might simply involve checking one or two other textbooks or asking a well-resourced and collegial colleague.

Am I likely to be teaching this material again in the near future?	If so, then additional time and effort may be reasonable, but, if you are unlikely to need to teach the topic again in the near future, then spending significant time on the resources may not be justifiable.
Do I have any similar resources for other topics that might provide a model I can adapt in the creation of a new resource?	If so, this may help to reduce the amount of time required to create the material. For example, if you need to curate a new collection of primary sources, you might look at another existing activity you have for another topic and use this as a basic template.

When considering your resources for a topic, it may also be useful to consider the following rule: if it takes more than 10-15 minutes of your time to collate, gather or create a resource, it should pay off over the foreseeable future. If, for example, you estimate that it will take you two hours to create a resource, but you are only likely to use that resource again once every few years, it may not be worth the time and effort. If, however, you estimate that it will take two hours of your time but that you are likely to use it every year for the next several years and it will be of higher quality than anything you have access to, the time may be more justifiable.

Growing in curriculum confidence

So, we have established that an important aim as you begin to teach is to steadily develop your curriculum confidence over time. As this grows, you may still rely heavily on "utilising" and "curating" from Diagram 6.1 to resource your lessons, but you should have a much richer understanding of why particular resources you find and curate are likely to be useful. You should also be becoming more skilled in adapting resources.

To bring this discussion to a close, what I am arguing is that your curriculum confidence is a crucial dimension of the quality of your work and the efficiency with which you get it done. Running after pre-prepared resources may assist you in the short term, but it is unlikely to eliminate your workload altogether. So, regardless of whether you utilise, curate or design material, remain focused on using these opportunities to develop and refine your curriculum confidence, because in the long-term, this will make the greatest difference.

Chapter summary

- Developing curriculum confidence is crucial to becoming an efficient and well-resourced history teacher and this takes time.
- When beginning to resource your units of work, it is generally best to collate and then create material.
- Collate material by consulting reputable sources such as strong textbooks in your faculty library and colleagues' resources that they have shared (never take these without asking and always acknowledge any material that you have been given).
- Ensure that effort you put in to creating resources is a reasonable use of your time.
- If you do create material, try to ensure that it can be scaled up and down (used over longer and shorter periods and with different class groups depending on how it is adapted and employed).

End of chapter questions

Questions for reflection and discussion	Questions to ask experienced teachers
1. How would you currently rate your own curriculum confidence? 2. Have you seen history teachers with strong curriculum confidence in operation in a school? What did they do that gave you the impression that they had this confidence?	1. What is your approach to designing units of work and gathering resources?

Further reading

Resource	Why bother reading it?
Robert Parkes, "Developing Your Approach to Teaching History", *Historical Thinking for History Teachers: A New Approach to Engaging Students and Developing Historical Consciousness*, Allen & Unwin, 2019, pp. 72–88	This chapter explores a range of key questions and issues that you will have to decide upon as you learn to teach secondary history.

Resource	Why bother reading it?
Megan Mansworth, *Teaching to the Top: Aiming High for Every Learner*, John Catt Educational, 2021 (Chapter 1: "Building the Foundations: Developing High-Level Subject Knowledge")	The first chapter of this book offers a refreshing discussion that places a teacher's subject knowledge and expertise at the centre of their teaching. Not only does this assist in teaching effectively, but it also nurtures a teacher's own enthusiasm for teaching. It is a good reminder that teaching should not simply be seen as a technocratic delivery process and that the ends are at least as important as the means.

CHAPTER 7

Learn to use curriculum documents

A key part of learning to develop your curriculum confidence as a secondary history teacher (see Chapter 6) involves using the curriculum documents you are required to work with. These documents will rarely set out exactly what needs to be done in a lesson-by-lesson structure. Overall, this is healthy in history because it gives teachers some freedom to teach topics in ways that are more flexible and interesting, but this does also mean that there is always effort required on the part of teachers.

Learning to *use* curriculum documents in secondary history involves developing the confidence to understand and interpret what is required for your particular class and using this to build an approach to the topics, knowledge and skills in focus. This flexibility is exciting, but it also can be daunting in the early stages of your career. Learning to accept that teaching is, in part, an interpretative process with in-built uncertainties and complexities is a crucial part of becoming a confident history teacher.

Platforms, not straitjackets

One of the most important principles to remember when teaching history underneath a formal curriculum document such as a syllabus is to make sure that you read it carefully and then use it; it should be a platform, not a straitjacket. This means paying attention to its key requirements (and ensuring that you meet them), identifying topic areas that you are more and less comfortable with (and then ensuring that you improve your knowledge and confidence in those areas that you are less familiar with), and looking for opportunities to breathe life into the subject. This includes finding interesting paths through the content that will give you opportunities to explore aspects of history that you think are the most important and enjoyable.

When you get to the point of looking closely at the topics you have (or opt) to teach, they will often include some kind of content outline such as a list of "content points" you will need to explore with the class. Sometimes this content outline will strike you as logically structured and helpful. In these cases you may be able to begin teaching at the top of the list and simply work your way down. In other cases, you may notice oddities in the way the content for a topic is outlined and determine that teaching the content points from top to bottom may not be the best approach. In the latter scenario, you still need to work within the framework you have been given but, provided there is no external examination that requires balanced coverage of the content, there is no reason why you cannot address the content points in whatever way you deem workable. This is a simple, but common, example of the teacher making use of the curriculum document rather than following it slavishly.

In scenarios where you are teaching history content that is to be examined by a high-stakes external exit examination (such as the Higher School Certificate at the end of Year 12 in New South Wales), this can become a little trickier, but the principle still generally holds: so long as you cover what is required, there should always be room to approach a curriculum document with some imagination and ingenuity.

Using curriculum documents

Some simple ways in which history teachers can begin to use rather than blindly follow curriculum documents in secondary history include:

- Where given an option, selecting topics to study that form a logical sequence within a course (more will be said on this in later chapters)
- Where given an option, selecting topics to study that you think will have a greater chance of bringing the subject to life for your students (this might be simply because you have more expertise in a particular area and believe that you will be able to do one topic more justice than another)
- Where given an option, selecting topics to study that you think will open up important ideas for your students to engage with
- Within a given topic, ensuring that the content is addressed/explored in a logical and meaningful manner (sometimes this may involve not simply teaching through a list of content points in the order that they appear in the curriculum document)
- Spending more time on some content points within a topic than others (more will also be said on this in a later chapter).

There are many ways to take charge of a curriculum document and use it to develop interesting and meaningful learning sequences, but this is a start.

Unfortunately, many of us currently operate in an educational culture that emphasises (and often rewards) compliance. It is obviously important to ensure that you always follow appropriate policies and procedures that you have agreed to in the education system or school that you work in, but cultures of compliance can also make people overly cautious and reluctant to take initiative. As your confidence in teaching history grows, so should your ability to work with curriculum documents in a manner that ensures that you meet their requirements but in a way that benefits your students and stays true to the discipline of history as much as possible. These documents will always have quirks and flaws that need to be countered with awareness, professionalism and willingness to take charge of the learning on behalf of your students and in the interests of their study of history.

In many of the following chapters, more practical approaches to using curriculum documents will be outlined. For now, it is enough to note that history is not a subject in which you can simply grab a curriculum document and follow it as though it were some kind of complete methodical recipe. Sometimes this can be disconcerting, particularly when you are new. But, like anything, the more you do it, the more comfortable you are likely to become. It makes sense, therefore, to start early.

Chapter summary

- Curriculum documents should be followed with professionalism.
- Most curriculum documents cannot simply be cut and pasted to make useable teaching programs; rather they need to be used to develop these.
- History teachers should read curriculum documents carefully and actively use them to ensure that what they teach is logical, coherent and as interesting as it can be within their particular school and class context.

End of chapter questions

Questions for reflection and discussion	Questions to ask experienced teachers
1. How well do you think that you understand the curriculum document (e.g., syllabus) that you are required to work with? 2. Which aspects of the curriculum document do you find the most difficult to understand and interpret?	1. What are some helpful pointers for interpreting and working with your curriculum document (syllabus)?

Further reading

Resource	Why bother reading it?
Robert Parkes, "Developing Your Approach to Teaching History", in *Historical Thinking for History Teachers: A New Approach to Engaging Students and Developing Historical Consciousness*, Allen & Unwin, 2019, pp. 72–88	This chapter explores a range of key questions and issues that you will have to decide upon as you learn to teach secondary history.
Kate Cameron and Jonathon Dallimore, "Making the Syllabus Work for You: Some Practical Tips for Approaching History in Stage 4–6", *Teaching History*, Vol. 54, No. 2, June 2020, pp. 25–32	The main aim of this brief article is to encourage teachers to think creatively and constructively with curriculum documents. It offers practical examples for teaching in an Australian context.

CHAPTER 8

Aim to engage, not entertain

There is no guarantee that the students you teach will enjoy history. This can pose a significant challenge since good history is ultimately demanding. It requires knowledge, patience, practice and time. If a student comes to your class with a positive and enthusiastic attitude towards history, this can be leveraged to help them make more rapid progress in the subject. If, however, they come with a negative attitude or opposition to the subject, it can make the task of teaching and learning the subject even more difficult. There is no point pretending otherwise.

There are many possible responses to this scenario. One might be to simply ignore the issue and stand firmly behind the belief that history is important and just needs to be learned regardless of whether the students think it is enjoyable.

Though this might seem callous at first, there is a simple truth to it: it can be dangerous for teachers, especially those new to the profession, to feel pressure to always make their subject enjoyable. Not only might this add to their workload, if students remain unmoved in their negative attitude to the subject, some teachers may be burdened by a sense of failure, and this could be disastrous for their sense of professional self-worth. To set universal enjoyment as a prerequisite for learning would be an irrationally high standard that few teachers would ever achieve.

Another response might be to look for ways to connect the topics and themes that you teach to issues that already interest your students and try to draw them into investment in the subject.[44] This seems intuitive to many teachers too and for good reason. We know that history can be fascinating, and we know that, even when people do not continue with history as a formal academic pursuit after school, many still engage enthusiastically with the past in varied

---

44 I am borrowing the term "investment" directly from James Durran, "Making the Investment", 24 July 2017: https://jamesdurran.blog/2017/07/24/making-the-investment/#more-1928

ways. Many of us also know from experience that teachers really can make potentially mundane material more interesting to students, even those who are not the most academically able. Fortunately, many (or perhaps enough) of my teachers certainly did this for me when I was a student.

Approaching engagement

For many reasons, this question of student "engagement" periodically returns as a controversy within the education community. Some have literally called for teachers to completely abandon the use of the term. Others have doubled down and said that in an age when teachers compete with video games, smart phones and artificial intelligence, engagement is more important than ever.

There is almost certainly no easy way to resolve this complex debate about engagement – and that is perfectly acceptable since education is complex and the neatest and tidiest solutions are often the most dangerous. There appear to be, however, more and less sensible ways to approach the issue that do not involve unproductively discarding the concept or setting up an unnecessarily burdensome standard requiring all of our lessons to be universally inspiring.

To start, it would be wise to consider at least four interconnected ideas relating to engagement: our goal, our strategies, our criteria and common obstacles. These are briefly outlined in Table 8.1.

TABLE 8.1: Important considerations for student engagement

Goal	The goal of engagement is not entertainment or even observable participation in activities. The goal should be to help students make genuine progress in the subject by developing their confidence. If students enjoy their time in a history class but learn nothing, then little is likely to have been gained.
Strategies	It is important to ensure that strategies that we use in the quest to engage students are not unreasonably taxing on teachers. If we spend several hours trying to create a 30-minute activity in the hope that students might enjoy the subject more, our teaching could rapidly become unsustainable.
Criteria	It is important to manage our own expectations around student engagement. If we set an unreasonably high bar for this – for example, that *all* students in the class must immediately enjoy the learning – then we could easily guarantee perpetual frustration.

Obstacles	It makes sense to take stock of common reasons that contribute to students' negative impressions of the subject and, in some cases, their resistance to participation and effort. Although we might try to eliminate unnecessary obstacles, we should also remember that not all resistance is equal. Sometimes, students simply do not like history because it is challenging, and it would be disastrous to remove all the challenging parts in order to increase student enjoyment.

What is the goal of engagement?

Without question, there is a danger that some discussions of engagement can lead to tacky forms of edutainment that could have questionable educational value. It is possible to accidentally slip into modes of entertainment in the hope that somehow students will learn something along the way.

The danger in this scenario is obvious enough: students' learning seems to have faded into the background and their short-term enthusiasm and enjoyment have become the central concerns.

If, however, the students' progress remains central to our project and the main goal in "engaging" them when they come to our classes, then we are less likely to fall into the trap of spending hours trying to catch their attention and only minutes using that attention to help them learn something meaningful.

So, from the outset, it is important to be clear on what the purpose of any attempt to engage our students is. As Chapter 5 argued, our ultimate goal as history teachers is to help students grow in their historical confidence and agility. If engagement is not a means to that meaningful end, then it runs the risk of becoming a distraction.

I should briefly note that I do not necessarily see any problem with teachers using humour, games and other strategies to create moments in which students take genuine pleasure in their class. Some teachers are more naturally humorous and entertaining, and they should not be discouraged from using these elements of their character so long as they do not become counter-productive. There are times and contexts in which this might need to be done with greater caution, but there are others in which it can become a more natural part of classroom culture.

Strategies for engagement

Once we have a clear goal in mind when we think of engagement, we then need to ask: what strategies would be reasonable to achieve those ends?

I recall a situation in my early years of teaching where to engage a class in the subject, I spent hours over a weekend planning an intricate game for them to play. We were launching into a series of lessons on the Easter Uprising in Ireland in 1916. So in the first lesson, we watched an excerpt from a documentary and conducted some overview reading to ensure that they understood the basic story. This failed to capture their attention in the way that I had hoped so, over a weekend, I spent hours planning a game for the students to play, hoping that this might excite them for the topic. The game was meant to be a fun challenge, but it was also designed to be educational in that it teased out a range of the key problems that the Irish nationalists faced in 1916, such as a lack of adequate resources to execute their plans.

I would estimate that three or four hours of planning went into the game, and I certainly enjoyed putting it together. In class, the game lasted for about one hour and most students seemed to enjoy it. It certainly helped capture their interest in the topic in a way that the documentary and the initial reading had not. In that narrow sense, the effort was worthwhile, but it was also taxing on my planning time as I essentially added a half-day of work to my already busy week. In exchange, I got just one hour of material that I never repeated again since it was the only time I ever taught the Easter Uprising. In hindsight, I consider the cost to have outweighed the benefit and I learned my lesson.

The point is that we have to be careful not to impose unnecessary burdens on ourselves as teachers in the pursuit of student interest. There is no way I could have created this kind of elaborate activity for every topic that I taught with every class. At that stage I did not even have my own children or many obligations outside of work. I would find it even harder now that I have a family of my own and other commitments.

To put this simply, I am suggesting that the strategies we use in the pursuit of student engagement, which I believe to be a broadly valid educational goal, must not overburden us as teachers such that we create an unsustainable workload. Our strategies must be realistic, and there may be times when we simply cannot spend too much time trying to find a way to make the material we must explore with a class more "interesting".

What I also learned from my 1916 Easter Uprising experience was that time-consuming activities like this may not even be necessary. In hindsight, I could have created a much simpler version of the game that would have taken me 15-20 minutes to plan instead of 3-4 hours. It is likely that it would have produced a similar outcome but taken far less of my time over a weekend.

Finally, experience in the classroom also suggests to me that sometimes students take time to develop interest in the material we explore as their knowledge and confidence grows, and this observation appears to be supported by some educational research.[45] On personal reflection, I am sure that I have developed a fascination for aspects of history that I thought I was not interested in only after developing richer knowledge about them. In other words, my interest followed my knowledge and confidence; it did not precede them. So, in many cases the best strategy for engaging students may not be spending inordinate amounts of time trying to create one or two fun activities, but getting started on the material so that the students' learning begins to progress.

Criteria for engagement

The third dimension of engagement that is important to consider is the criteria we use for our own success. Do we expect *all* students in the class to be immediately thrilled by our attempts to pique their interest? If so, it is likely to be a recipe for frustration. I am certain that even the most widely interesting activities I have created and planned still failed to grab some students' attention or interest.

So, even though I may hope that all students become interested in the topics that I teach, it would be foolish to be overly critical of my teaching if I do not reach that dream. Some students will never be interested in the history I teach, regardless of my best efforts to convince them that it is fascinating and important. I cannot stop teaching and wait for them to be interested before proceeding; that would be both bizarre and dangerous.

Also, some students do not register their engagement through overt expressions of enthusiasm, so immediate responses to our lessons can be a misleading proxy for interest. I distinctly recall thinking that a class was deeply uninspired by my teaching of the First World War, only to find out mid-way through the topic that it was their favourite so far. Though their outward signs were not of bursting enthusiasm, when asked, they were clearly interested, and the more substantial work they began submitting as the topic progressed was of a much better standard than I had initially expected.

Obstacles to engagement

Lastly, it is worth trying to develop a realistic outlook on what obstacles there are to student engagement in history. Not only might this help you to avoid those obstacles where reasonable to do so, but it might also help you to be less

---

[45] Daniel Willingham, *Why Don't Students Like School? (2nd Ed.)*, Jossey-Bass, 2021, pp. 9–10.

critical of yourself, since sometimes certain topics or aspects of history are simply less enjoyable than others.

In Australia, for example, it is common for students to find many aspects of national history less immediately appealing. Teachers in many states report similar groans of concern when they say to a class: "Today we will begin a new topic on the Federation of Australia." Many students report too much repetition in Australian history material over the course of their primary and secondary education. Regardless of whether these reports are accurate reflections of the curriculum, they do mean that many students come to school with a negative impression of what it means to study aspects of Australian history.[46] In many contexts, it is a real obstacle.

Some students may have also developed negative impressions of history from earlier experiences in primary and secondary school. They may, for example, have been taught by a primary teacher with much stronger ability to bring other subject areas to life, such as science or literature, leaving the student with a duller experience of history (the reverse may also be true). Or, they may have been taught history in earlier years of secondary school by a non-specialist teacher who found teaching the subject difficult. Even if the experience was not particularly negative, they still may not arrive in history classes in later years with an enthusiastic expectation of what the subject involves and they may take some time to be won over.

If students have not received strong instruction in history prior to arriving at your class, some may also lack confidence in their ability. This may mean that they are less willing to make an effort or contribute to class activities, which can easily form another initial barrier to their enthusiasm for the subject. Students such as this may take more time to develop their confidence, and this cannot be rushed.

Obstacles such as these can present additional challenges for teachers who are keen to share their enthusiasm for a subject they are genuinely passionate about. It can be deflating to teach several classes at once in which some students hold negative impressions of the subject or are resistant to making an effort in it from the beginning.

This is not uncommon and, as teachers, we are faced with some difficult choices about how to proceed when students, or indeed entire classes, arrive with negative impressions of our subject. Perhaps most crucially, we

---

46 Anna Clark, *History's Children: History Wars in the Classroom*, University of New South Wales Press, 2008, and, more recently, Anna Clark, "Teaching and Learning Difficult Histories" in Epstein, T., and Peck, C., (eds.) *Teaching and Learning Difficult Histories in International Contexts: A Critical Sociocultural Approach*, Routledge, 2019, pp. 82–94.

cannot expect to win over all students who have had negative experiences with history in a short time. Unrealistic expectations in this area can also be deflating.

A sensible approach?

With the above discussion in mind, I generally treat student engagement as one aspect of my teaching. That is, I take it seriously, but I do not treat it as the most important concern. Personally, I have always tried to look for ways to communicate the joy and interest I find in history and I aim to help my students enjoy the challenge of the subject. I try to bring history to life by telling interesting stories and by finding questions, sources and activities that might pique their interest or deepen their curiosity. I try to bring out the drama of primary documents when I read them aloud with the students and pause documentaries as we are watching them to make interesting connections with other material we have explored. I also try to stimulate and direct interesting discussions and debates that are lively and find opportunities to open history up for student choice and freedom. All of this, however, is done so that students can learn something new, consider an issue from a new perspective, and extend their confidence as participants in discussions about the past.

Chapter summary

- Student engagement can be a contested feature of teaching and learning.
- Extreme responses to student engagement can be unhelpful in either dismissing it as an important dimension of teaching or setting unrealistic expectations that all a teacher's lessons must explode with excitement.
- Engagement should not be seen as synonymous with entertainment.
- Reflecting genuinely on the goals, strategies, criteria and obstacles surrounding student engagement can help sharpen a teacher's focus on its place within their planning and teaching.

End of chapter questions

Questions for reflection and discussion	Questions to ask experienced teachers
1. What aspects of history did you find most/least interesting at school? 2. Why is engagement not the same as "entertainment"? 3. What are some common problems associated with engagement?	1. How do you approach student engagement in your current teaching context? 2. What do you do to try to make less-interesting parts of the syllabus more enjoyable for students?

Further reading

Resource	Why bother reading it?
James Durran, "Making the Investment", 24 July 2017: https://jamesdurran.blog/2017/07/24/making-the-investment/#more-1928	This short blog post offers a helpful way of thinking about student engagement that is practical and avoids confusing engagement with entertainment.
Tom Sherrington, "TPS6: How Do I Engage Passive Learners?", 17 January 2023: https://teacherhead.com/2023/01/17/tps6-how-do-i-engage-passive-learners/	Tom Sherrington's blog includes many practical pieces on specific and common classroom challenges. In this post, he discusses how he approaches situations when students are disengaged or resist making an effort.

Part Two
Planning — Year Levels and Topics

CHAPTER 9

Balance clarity, direction and flexibility

In the busy life of a school teacher, clarity and direction can be powerful tools to embed through planning. Selecting and justifying topics when there is room to do so, agreeing on major assessment tasks with colleagues that establish long-range learning goals, and possessing a sense of how topics will broadly progress as you begin teaching them can all be helpful to lean on when school life gets busier.

At the same time, teachers need to be flexible. In fact, if you have an element of perfectionism in your personality as I do, teaching can be additionally challenging since nothing seems to ever work strictly to plan. You thought you had six lessons to work through a particular part of a topic, and then you lose a lesson to a fire drill. You thought you had four lessons to work through another section of a topic because the swimming carnival was scheduled for Friday, but it was then cancelled at the last minute because of poor weather, so you need to come up with an additional lesson. You were planning to do an in-class writing task on Thursday, but the students "forgot" to tell you that half were booked in for a music excursion to see a show in the city that day. Disruption is a feature of schooling; it is not necessarily a bug.

Herein lies one of the many paradoxes of teaching: careful planning is enormously powerful, but teachers always need to remain flexible. Planning that is too open-ended can be messy, but overly rigid planning can cause undue stresses of its own.

Clarity and direction

Broader strategic planning for teaching secondary history can set you up to handle the challenge of managing several classes and balancing this with the other activities of a busy school teacher's life. Selecting your topics for the year, creating the major assessment tasks for each class, and having a general sense of how classes should progress through each topic will mean that aspects of teaching and learning can develop momentum as each term gathers pace.

If, for example, you are teaching a topic on the Russian Revolution and you know that the students will need to produce an essay towards the end that makes an argument about the relative importance of different causal factors explaining the triumph of the Bolsheviks, then both you and the students know where the learning is going and can discuss this as the topic progresses. If you are teaching a class exploring imperial China and the major assessment task is to deliver an oral presentation assessing the historical significance of one individual in a particular period, then both you and the class have a shared understanding of where the learning is going, and this can become an open and natural part of discussions as lessons move forward.

As your confidence grows and you have taught certain topics a few times, some of this direction and momentum becomes natural, but it is important in the early stages of your career to be conscious of this high-level planning and take it seriously.

In many contexts, something as basic as a general scope and sequence will help provide some clarity to your planning. These usually identify what topics will be taught throughout a year or semester, in what order these will be taught, how long each topic will take, and any major assessment tasks that will be completed in the same period. Scope and sequences are helpful for individual teachers, but especially useful when there are several teachers working with classes in the same age-group and course.

Constraints on planning and direction

In some year levels that you teach, the direction of the learning will be constrained significantly by other factors that you have little to no control over, such as external examinations. You might also be working in a setting where the faculty you are part of has already decided the major assessment tasks for the year group you are teaching, since there are multiple classes completing the same course (there might be five Year 10 history classes, for example). In other scenarios, you might be relatively free to decide on the direction a course or topic takes. Of course, you may also find yourself in a situation in which you are teaching a range of classes, some with tight constraints and others with relatively few.

TABLE 9.1: Different scenarios influencing the direction of your planning

External examinations	If you are teaching a year group that is working towards major external examinations, the direction of the learning will be largely imposed on you. You should ensure that you are familiar with the examination requirements and make these an explicit part of the teaching and learning across the topics you teach.
Faculty/school requirements	Even in situations where there are no external examinations, schools may insist on end-of-year or end-of-semester exams for every subject and every year level. In this scenario, the faculty may then be required to set an examination, and this will form part of the constraints on your teaching. Even without end-of-year examinations, a faculty may decide that, for the sake of consistency, every class will complete the same major assessment tasks across a course to ensure equity, and this will constrain aspects of your teaching and set some of the direction for your planning.
Greater freedom	In other scenarios, you may be working in a school as the only history teacher and may have much more freedom setting assessments. You may have much greater scope to be creative in this scenario and decide to try different approaches. You may, of course, decide to use more common assessment approaches because you have seen these work well. The opportunity to experiment does not always mean that things *should* be done in a radically different way.

The important point is that, whether imposed or chosen, developing a clear sense of direction can help create momentum for you and the students across topics and across whole courses more generally. Though I would argue that this helps at any stage of your career, it is particularly important when you are newer to the profession.

Flexibility

No matter how constrained you are in your role or in a particular topic, you still need to remain flexible. Schools may need to adjust assessment weeks and bring forward or push back examination blocks. Part-way through a course, your faculty supervisor might need to adjust a common assessment task that was set at the beginning of term because of a complication. On a smaller scale too, it is wise to expect that, at some point, some disruption will require you to pivot and adjust your plan for one or some of your classes.

Given all these possibilities, it helps to ensure that your planning is not so rigid that it cannot absorb these changes or allow you to make alterations without causing too much stress. Anecdotally, it seems that agility is one of the key survival traits of veteran teachers.

To take one concrete example of what flexibility might look like in reality: I rarely plan sequences of learning around a specific number of lessons. Instead, I tend to allocate a lesson range to the sequence so that I am not locked into a rigid number for the sequence to be effective. Rather than planning to work through a sequence in five lessons, for example, I might plan to work through it in four to six lessons and give myself some room to move. If the class moves quicker and is free of disruption, I can complete the sequence in four to five lessons. If, however, they move slower than expected or I lose a lesson unexpectedly, I can extend this to six and my plans have not been ruined.

In addition, there are times when the joy of teaching and learning involves moving away from following a rigid plan. Some research suggests, and my own experience would affirm, that students often respond positively to teachers with the confidence to follow unexpected ideas and questions but retain coherent overall direction in their teaching.[47] This becomes easier over time as your experience grows and once you have taught a topic several times. The confidence to be agile like this can certainly make teaching more enjoyable and less stressful.

Through the following chapters other suggestions about planning will continue to argue that clarity is crucial, but that rigidity is best avoided. The advice will attempt to capture what we might call "flexible clarity" in our planning of whole topics, smaller sequences and individual lessons too.

Chapter summary

- Clear planning helps ensure that teaching history moves in a constructive direction and helps give the diverse students in your classes a sense of where their learning is headed.
- Schools can, however, be unpredictable places, and teachers always need to be ready to adapt and adjust.
- As you grow in confidence, adjusting is likely to become easier, but it is best to begin with the assumption that learning to be flexible is a requirement of the job.

---

47 Pedro de Bruyckere, Paul Kirschner and Yvonne Xian-han Huang, "Authentic Teachers: Student Criteria Perceiving the Authenticity of Teachers", *Cogent Education*, Vol. 3, No. 1, 2016, pp. 1–15.

End of chapter questions

Questions for reflection and discussion	Questions to ask experienced teachers
1. Why is clear planning important to teaching? 2. Why is flexibility important to teaching? 3. Why are clarity and flexibility not mutually exclusive aspects of planning?	1. Have you ever had to make major adjustments to your teaching part-way through a course? What happened? 2. How do you remain flexible even when you have clear plans for your classes?

Further reading

Resource	Why bother reading it?
Robert Marzano, *The Art and Science of Teaching: A Comprehensive Framework for Effective Instruction*, Association for Supervision and Curriculum Development, 2007 (Chapter 10: "What Will I Do to Develop Effective Lessons Organized into a Cohesive Unit", pp. 174–90)	Marzano's book offers a range of practical ideas for approaching teaching. This chapter sets out helpful tips to ensure that the "infrastructure" planned for approaching topics and lessons is logical and helpful. Although the ideas are not history-specific, many of the principles provide helpful direction for planning teaching and learning in history classes.

CHAPTER 10

Use, adapt or plan thoughtful topic sequences

In most education jurisdictions, teachers are bound to varying degrees by curriculum documents. For history these will often include a mixture of mandatory content and areas in which the school and/or teacher might select from a list of options or create their own – some lean more towards the former (in which case planning should be relatively easy) and others lean more towards the latter (in which case more extensive planning may be required). If it is the case in your jurisdiction that you are required to make some selections in the content for your history courses (or create them), it can be daunting but it need not be overwhelming.

Confident and experienced history teachers probably have greater freedom when there are topic options within a curriculum. They are likely to have deeper knowledge and experience, so switching between topic areas may be less demanding on time and energy. Less-experienced teachers of history are likely to find this more challenging since new topic areas can mean more preparation, more background reading, and more resource collation and creation.

In general, less-experienced teachers should be encouraged to lean on the expertise of others as they begin to plan their approaches to teaching and learning. If possible, find a more experienced history teacher in your school or local area or professional association who can provide some advice, resources and directions on topics that you are not familiar with. In doing this, the idea is not to mimic a more experienced teacher, but to learn from them as you nurture your own curriculum confidence.

Using, or more likely adapting, units of work someone else has created with your own classes can be a valuable way to cut down on planning time so long as these have been shared or made available and so long as you acknowledge your sources. It is also important to remember the warnings in Chapter 6 about simply grabbing readily available material and trying to "implement" it without much thought.

Play to your strengths and grow into freedom

Even though you ultimately should aim to select topics thoughtfully, there comes a point at which you will need to stop agonising over selection and make a decision. It may be best to go with what you have most material to teach or what you are most familiar with – play to your strengths to save time and energy. Hopefully, with some guidance, you will be able to develop a reasonable sequence of topics, themes and issues within your course that is logical and helps students build their historical confidence and agility.

For those with more experience, time or confidence, choice can be one of the most exciting aspects of the job. It opens up opportunities to put together interesting curriculum sequences, draw more deeply on recent historical scholarship, experiment with new themes, and possibly even meet the interests of a class more directly. Even experienced teachers, however, need to be careful that experimentation with new topics and material does not lead to burnout and unnecessary demands of finding and creating new resources.

Freedom is exciting and it can certainly enrich teaching programs and contribute to job satisfaction, but it can also make for heavier workloads. Sometimes it can make sense to teach a topic option for several years to avoid additional work of planning and preparation. It is not necessarily laziness or lack of professional enthusiasm that might lead someone to teach the same topic for several years straight even if the option to change is available.

Coming to grips with Russia

Since my undergraduate degree in history, I have developed a deep interest in Russian and early Soviet history – particular the period leading up to the Second World War. I had wonderful teachers of this material during my degree and then eventually an excellent teacher-mentor in a school who had taught this material for many years.

When I first began teaching senior modern history (Year 11 and 12), I had the option to choose many different aspects of 20th century history to explore with my classes. Given my continuing interest in Russian and Soviet history, I decided to focus on this as one of the areas we would explore. I never stopped teaching the Russian and Soviet options because, as my depth of knowledge grew, I was better able to translate that into interesting and useful teaching and learning experiences in my classroom without massive investments of time. Becoming much more confident in this one area of modern history then also gave me a kind of template for teaching other topics because I knew what it was like to be deeply comfortable with a particular area of history. I do not believe that it was unprofessional or lazy of me to teach the same topic year in, year out even when I had the option to change. In fact, I would argue that it was the opposite – it helped me enrich my knowledge of the past and how to teach it more effectively, and that now helps immeasurably when I am required to teach newer topics that I am not so familiar with.

There are two important observations to draw out at this point. First, if you are less confident with teaching history and are faced with topic choices, use existing material or the expertise of others to guide your choices and cut down on unnecessary planning and preparation where possible. Second, as your curriculum confidence grows (see Chapter 6), begin to look for opportunities to adjust this as may be required.

Rationalising your topic choices

It is always worth being able to explain why you are exploring a particular topic with your students. This is not so that you can defensively justify it to them, but so that you can communicate clearly why you think it is important and where it fits into broader aspects of the course that you are teaching. Sometimes, the answer to the question "Why are we learning this?" might come down to a simple: "Because it is mandatory". But it would be ideal to have something more to say about each topic's rationale and purpose, even just for the clarity this may help to provide for you as the teacher. Some students may not ultimately agree with your rationalisations, but it would be impossible to please all the students you teach all of the time – that is an unrealistic goal in most educational settings.

TABLE 10.1: Clarifying logical paths through curriculum

Chronological	Do not underestimate the power of narrative in history – it is, after all, a subject fundamentally shaped by stories. Sometimes, curriculum options might allow you to select topics that develop a broader sense of chronology across a period of time. For example, you may opt to complete a topic on the Meiji Restoration in Japan followed by an exploration of the Second World War in the Pacific or a study of Nazi Germany following a topic on the First World War. These would allow students to follow a broader flow of history across time.

Thematic	Sometimes, topic options might allow you to establish some intelligent comparative work across a key theme (or set of themes). For example, you might study imperial China followed by the Roman Empire, allowing you to pose interesting and useful questions about empires as a core theme of the topics. You might opt to study the French Revolution followed by the Russian Revolution, making "revolution" an underlying theme of the topics.
Ethical	For good reason, many history teachers have become more concerned over recent decades to ensure that their classes are introduced to a wider variety of topics and perspectives. Where and how do the histories of women or minority groups feature in a history curriculum? Some topics from a curriculum document may lend themselves to exploring questions about gender, civil rights and contemporary concerns, and this may factor into a teacher's decision when it comes to planning a path through the curriculum.
Conceptual	You might also plan topics around specific disciplinary concepts to help students explore aspects of historical thinking in more depth. For example, you could frame a topic around the concept of causation and interpretations and focus most of the students' attention on those themes. Their major assessment task might then require them to communicate about issues relating to causation within the topic. Another topic might foreground the ability to work with a variety of historical sources, and the major assessment task might concentrate on this aspect of history.

It should be remembered that there is probably no watertight path through any history curriculum. You are likely to always have wanted to cover this or that theme or issue but not had the time, or the topics may not have aligned perfectly to allow you to do so. The question is not whether your curriculum path was perfect, but whether it was thoughtful. As you continue to teach and remain reflective, you can then improve this over time, and that is all that can be asked of anyone beginning their teaching career.

Chapter summary

- History curriculum documents can allow (or even require) you to make choices about the topics, themes and issues you explore with your classes.
- Although the freedom of choice may be exciting, it can also be daunting.

- When faced with curriculum choices, consider what you already know and are confident with and what resources might be available to you (through a colleague at your school, for example).
- If you have time and the inclination, be creative with your topic options, but make sure that these can be communicated to the students, parents and colleagues.
- There is nothing wrong with teaching the same topic over many consecutive years to develop confidence and expertise. Do not feel pressure to keep changing topics simply because this appears to be the creative or entertaining path.

End of chapter questions

Questions for reflection and discussion	Questions to ask experienced teachers
1. Why is planning coherent sequences of topics important in secondary history? 2. What areas of the history curriculum that you are required to teach are you most/least confident with?	1. How do you make sure that the topics that you teach form a coherent whole across a course or year?

Further reading

Resource	Why bother reading it?
Kate Cameron and Jonathon Dallimore, "Making the Syllabus Work for You: Some Practical Tips for Approaching History in Stage 4–6", *Teaching History*, Vol. 54, No. 2, June 2020, pp. 25–32	This article outlines some ways of remaining in charge of the syllabus as you meet its requirements to teach history in secondary settings.
Dale Banham, "Raising Attainment", in Davies, I. (ed.) *Debates in History Teaching*, Routledge, 2017, pp. 215–26	Banham's chapter in *Debates in History Teaching* includes a range of practical tips covering various aspects of secondary history, including reading, research, developing arguments, developing vocabulary and communication. His discussion in this chapter is centred on the question: "How do we develop a culture of excellence?" Part of his answer includes a consideration of how to frame and connect the topics we teach.

Resource	Why bother reading it?
Catherine Priggs, "No More 'Doing' Diversity", *Teaching History*, No. 179, June 2020	This article outlines ways in which one history department diversified their curriculum choices to broaden the coverage of issues and perspectives included across their history courses.
Kay Traille, *Hearing Their Voices: Teaching History to Students of Color*, Rowman and Littlefield, 2019	Traille's research provides important insights into the considerations that history teachers need to prioritise when teaching diverse students.
Emily Folorunsho and Laura Gladwin, *Succeeding as a History Teacher*, Bloomsbury, 2024 (Chapter 3: "A Diverse Curriculum")	Emily Folorunsho's discussion of diversity within history curriculum offers excellent advice on ensuring that the themes, issues, scales, resources and perspectives explored in secondary history are both intentional and appropriately varied.

CHAPTER 11

Do not treat all content as equal

When you are teaching secondary history topics that are not assessed by higher-stakes external exams, there can often be more flexibility in what you teach, how long you spend exploring aspects of topics, and how long you spend covering some topics in general. In these settings, teachers should have some freedom to spend more and less time on different aspects of the topics they teach. It should be noted that this may need to be negotiated with a head of faculty or colleagues teaching the same year group.

When this is the case, a useful principle to work with is that it is important to avoid treating all content as equal. You may, and indeed should, plan to spend more time on aspects of a topic that will be more fruitful and interesting to give your units of work greater chance of academic rigour and appeal among the students. In Australia, for example, in Year 7, students are often required to study "ancient civilisations" in which they explore several key themes. These typically include:

1. The geographic setting of the civilisation
2. Key social groups within the civilisation
3. Nature of contact with external societies (such as trade and warfare)
4. A significant individual
5. The ancient civilisation's legacy.

If I have eight weeks to teach these five major components and there are no high-stakes external examinations, I know from a quick glance which of the five themes I will be spending more time on than others. I certainly will not be spending four of the eight weeks exploring the geography of ancient China in gruelling detail. It is certainly possible to do that, and there are fascinating questions exploring the degree to which geography shapes political and social developments.[48] In the context of Year 7, however, my guess is that this is not

---

[48] See, for example, Tim Marshall, *Prisoners of Geography: Ten Maps That Tell You Everything You Need to Know about Global Politics*, Elliot and Thompson Limited, 2016.

the most interesting or, I would argue, important theme to explore, especially considering that the class may be studying history as a separate subject for the first time.

Instead, in the example provided above, I would be far more likely to spend more time on components two, three and four of this topic, because I know that they offer excellent opportunities to develop substantive and disciplinary knowledge and because I know from experience that students generally respond well to these. So, if I have eight weeks for the topic, I might break it down in the manner set out in Table 11.1.

TABLE 11.1: A rough breakdown of a Year 7 unit on ancient China

Week	Theme(s)
Week 1 (3 lessons)	Introduction and geographic setting
Week 2 (3 lessons)	Key social groups within ancient China
Week 3 (3 lessons)	
Week 4 (3 lessons)	Nature of contact with external societies
Week 5 (3 lessons)	
Week 6 (3 lessons)	A significant individual
Week 7 (3 lessons)	
Week 8 (3 lessons)	Ancient China's legacies

Note that the introduction to the unit only receives three lessons in total. That means there is likely to be only one or two lessons on the geographic setting. There are, however, six lessons allocated to each of the following: social groups, nature of contact, and significant individual. There are then only three lessons allocated to the legacies aspect of the topic. I have planned to spend more time on some aspects of the topic than others, provided I have the freedom to do so.

This takes us back to Chapter 7 ("Learn to use curriculum documents"). If I were to treat all content as equal, I would not really be *using* my curriculum document; I would be slavishly following it, and that could impact my teaching negatively.

Chapter summary

- When there are no external examinations that require teachers to work through every aspect of a given topic thoroughly, teachers will hopefully be given some freedom to emphasise some aspects of the topics they teach over others.
- To decide which aspects to spend more time on, consider which elements will provide the best opportunities to develop the students' substantive and disciplinary knowledge.
- A secondary consideration should be which aspects of a topic the students are most likely (not guaranteed) to enjoy more than others.

End of chapter questions

Questions for reflection and discussion	Questions to ask experienced teachers
1. Re-examine Table 11.1. In what other possible ways could this material be structured to place emphasis on different areas of the topic? 2. Using the curriculum document that you will be required to teach in your jurisdiction, select one or two topics. How might you break these down into a basic teaching plan like that outlined in Table 11.1?	1. When there are no external exams for the material you are teaching, how do you decide what content to spend more and less time on?

Further reading

Resource	Why bother reading it?
Robert Marzano, *The Art and Science of Teaching: A Comprehensive Framework for Effective Instruction*, Association for Supervision and Curriculum Development, 2007 (Chapter 10: "What Will I do to Develop Effective Lessons Organized into a Cohesive Unit", pp. 174–90)	Marzano's book offers a range of practical ideas for approaching teaching. This chapter sets out helpful tips to ensure that the "infrastructure" planned for approaching topics and lessons is logical and helpful. Although the ideas are not history-specific, many of the principles provide helpful direction for planning teaching and learning in history classes.

CHAPTER 12

Break each topic into manageable parts

I remember beginning new topics when I was in my early years of teaching. I would calculate how many lessons I had available to cover the content, and it could be overwhelming. I might, for example, have had eight weeks to cover a topic on Australia in the Cold War period with Year 10 at the pace of four one-hour lessons per week. The math was simple: four eights are 32. I had 32 lessons to plan, and that was just one of six classes I was teaching at the time. This "individual lesson view" of the units I was teaching was crushing.

TABLE 12.1: An example of the individual lesson view of a unit

Week 1				Week 2				Week 3				Week 4				Week 5				Week 6				Week 7				Week 8			
1	2	3	4	1	2	3	4	1	2	3	4	1	2	3	4	1	2	3	4	1	2	3	4	1	2	3	4	1	2	3	4

Parts of a whole, not isolated fragments

I had probably already been shown this, but for some reason it took me a few attempts at planning and delivering new units of work to put the individual lesson view aside and replace it with a system that broke the unit into several major components to guide me and the students through the topic. Instead of thinking about individual lessons as the starting point of a unit of work – building a unit of work from the lesson up – I began to think of the larger components of the unit as the starting point – building down to the individual lessons. This involved asking several questions about the unit of work before I really began to think about individual lessons. These were:

- What is my overall aim in the unit of work?
- What are the major components/themes that the unit of work needs to cover?

- What kinds of resources and activities will I need for these components?
- What will individual lessons look like?

This was a more top-down rather than lesson-up view of units of work in which the lessons simply fill up the parts and the parts flow together and fill up the topic. I was no longer thinking about 32 individual bits of a unit, but 5–6 major components, and this seemed much more manageable.

TABLE 12.2: Units of work as components rather than individual lessons

Week 1	Week 2	Week 3	Week 4	Week 5	Week 6	Week 7	Week 8
Intro	Component 1	Component 2		Component 3		Component 4	Conclusion
2–3 lessons	4–5 lessons	5–6 lessons		7–8 lessons		5–6 lessons	3–4 lessons

Week 1	Week 2	Week 3	Week 4	Week 5	Week 6	Week 7	Week 8
Intro	The global Cold War	Australian responses to communism		Australia in the Vietnam War (military history)		Australia in the Vietnam War (social history)	Conclusion
2–3 lessons	4–5 lessons	5–6 lessons		7–8 lessons		5–6 lessons	3–4 lessons

Once I learned to break units of work down into their major components, planning the individual lessons was much quicker, since I just needed to plan a sequence of lessons for each component. It also meant that as I began to move through the unit and became busier and more tired throughout a term, I was not keeping track of 32 individual lessons but thinking about where I was up to in each component. If I took care of each component, I knew the components would take care of the topic, because I had planned it as such.

Sometimes your curriculum document may indicate these components of a topic clearly and logically and you simply have to identify and teach through them. Other times, the way a topic is laid out in a curriculum document may require more effort on your part to break it down into major components. Either way, the important point is that you begin to move away from an atomised approach to planning your teaching which results in lesson after lesson after lesson after lesson. Instead, divide the topic into some major themes or areas and then consider what lessons will be most appropriate for each one.

If you work towards a cumulative goal in each section of a topic, this will make the process of moving through the major components of a topic even clearer for both you and the students. The following two chapters should be considered directly alongside this idea, and should help you to infuse each of your topics and each of their main components with greater meaning and clarity.

Natural flow

An additional benefit of planning the bulk of your teaching in secondary history across topics and components rather than individual lessons is that you are likely to create more natural flow in the learning. Instead of each lesson feeling like a completely new beginning, students are more likely to get a sense that their efforts and learning have come from somewhere and are moving in a logical direction.

Not only does this make it easier to communicate the main ideas and avoid the atomisation of learning, but it also allows you as the teacher to build natural flow into the lessons. If, for example, you plan a topic by setting out four or five main components to work through, as you begin to move through each, you can refer back to a larger story and a set of larger questions that sit underneath the lessons. You can also begin lessons easily by referring back to previous learning and clearly explaining how the students will continue to build on prior efforts.

There is also an important reality to this: in the real life of teaching in a school, content and skills often require more than one individual lesson to work through thoroughly. In addition, this means that the overall learning goal might need to be broken down into several lessons. One clear example of this in secondary history is essay-writing, which often needs more than a single lesson to be meaningful. In the first lesson, the students might read a high-quality sample essay and deconstruct its key strengths. In the second lesson, they might then discuss possible responses to one or two new questions and roughly draft the outline of a response. In the third lesson, they might begin writing a complete response to a new question that will be submitted to the teacher for feedback. If an observer only saw one of these lessons, they might think that the teaching approach lacked something, but that is because one individual lesson is insufficient for the deep learning required. The individual lessons only really make sense when considered within a larger whole.

Chapter summary

- Most topics you are required to teach in secondary history can be broken into major components.
- Use these larger components to group together sequences of lessons that help guide you and the students through the topic.

End of chapter questions

Questions for reflection and discussion	Questions to ask experienced teachers
1. What are the key problems with taking a "lesson view" of planning in secondary history? 2. What advantages are there to breaking a topic into smaller components?	1. How do you generally plan to teach new topics?

Further reading

Resource	Why bother reading it?
Dale Banham, "Raising Attainment", in Davies, I. (ed.) *Debates in History Teaching*, Routledge, 2017, pp. 215–26	Banham's chapter in *Debates in History Teaching* includes a range of practical tips covering various aspects of secondary history, including reading, research, developing arguments, developing vocabulary and communication. His discussion in this chapter is centred on the question: "How do we develop a culture of excellence?" Part of his answer includes a consideration of how to frame and connect the topics we teach.
Robert Marzano, *The Art and Science of Teaching: A Comprehensive Framework for Effective Instruction*, Association for Supervision and Curriculum Development, 2007 (Chapter 10: "What Will I Do to Develop Effective Lessons Organized into a Cohesive Unit", pp. 174–90)	Marzano's book offers a range of practical ideas for approaching teaching. This chapter sets out helpful tips to ensure that the "infrastructure" planned for approaching topics and lessons is logical and helpful. Although the ideas are not history-specific, many of the principles provide helpful direction for planning teaching and learning in history classes.

CHAPTER 13

Work towards smaller and larger cumulative goals

In the previous chapter, we discussed the importance of breaking each topic that you teach in secondary history into major components. The number of these components may vary depending on the amount of time you have to work through the topic, how old the students are, and other factors. In almost all cases, however, breaking a topic into smaller parts will help clarify where each lesson fits into the larger whole, and will help you and the students keep track of where you are up to in the learning.

It also helps your planning, resource collation/creation, and time management if you ensure that you work towards a cumulative goal for the whole topic and also smaller cumulative goals for each component of the topic. That is, at the end of each of the main components of the topic, plan for the students to complete a larger task to synthesise and communicate their understanding of what they have learned and then plan for them to complete something larger again towards the end of the whole topic.

Ideally, these smaller cumulative goals will feed directly into the larger cumulative goals of the topic. For example, if the students will need to write an entire essay at the end of the unit, the smaller cumulative goals for each part of the topic should build towards this so that the students develop their confidence and are given several significant opportunities to present work for feedback and guidance.

Some examples

If, for example, we were required to teach a six-week topic to Year 10 on the First World War, preparing students to sit an examination in which they would need to respond to source-based questions, we might break the topic down into the sequence outlined in Table 13.1 (depending on exactly what the curriculum document required).

TABLE 13.1: Cumulative goals throughout a unit of work on the First World War

Week 1	Week 2	Week 3	Week 4	Week 5	Week 6
Intro	Causes of WW1	Key campaigns/battles	Home fronts		Peace/legacy
Quiz	Written explanation using sources	Source analysis questions	Group presentations (home front sources)		Written explanation
Overall task: First World War topic test (source-based exam questions)					

The overall task in this example will be a topic test including source-based questions. So, as the class moves through each of the major components of the topic, the students develop their substantive, disciplinary and practical knowledge relevant to this larger task. They also demonstrate their progress in these areas in a substantial manner at the end of each component so that they are building towards the overall task of the unit. These smaller cumulative tasks may be something that the students submit for direct teacher feedback, but you may not require everything to be formally submitted. Later chapters will discuss different strategies for providing feedback to students.

The same approach could also work if students of a similar age were working on a different topic but were required to write a longer essay as the overall task linked to the topic. If that topic were the Cold War, our approach to this scenario might look like the outline in Table 13.2.

TABLE 13.2: Cumulative goals throughout a unit of work on the Cold War

Week 1	Week 2	Week 3	Week 4	Week 5	Week 6	Week 7	Week 8
Intro	The global Cold War	Australian responses to communism	Australia in the Vietnam War (military history)		Australia in the Vietnam War (social history)		Conclusion
Quiz	Sample essay deconstruction	Quiz and complete essay introduction	Essay plan and one complete body paragraph		Draft essay (intro, 3 body paragraphs and a conclusion)		Structured debate
Overall task: Extended essay response							

In this second example, the overall task for the topic is an extended essay including the standard introduction, body paragraphs and conclusion. So, we might begin in early components of the topic by deconstructing a full sample essay to ensure that the students see a clear and quality example of the end goal. We might then continue in the next section by requiring the students to write an introduction to an essay using a model or scaffold provided to ensure that they are confident with the requirements of this aspect of essay-writing. After providing feedback on this, we might then move on to writing and providing feedback on body paragraphs and towards the end get them to draft a complete essay. By the time the students are required to write their final essay response to the overall assessment task, they will have had plenty of practice and received lots of specific feedback on their work to ensure that they have had the opportunity to improve.

Deciding what is most important to learn and remember

One of the most important points about planning these cumulative tasks is that they will help you make fundamental decisions about the students' learning as you move through each part of a topic. Your teaching can then be more responsive to how the students are progressing, because you should have a clearer idea about what they need to know and do. In other words, these cumulative goals will help you answer the question: "What do students really need to know and remember for this part of the topic?" When you plan small revision and consolidation activities (such as a quiz or class discussion), this will help you decide what to ask the students to recall so that you can check on their knowledge and understanding of ideas and information that will be crucial to the cumulative goal.

When I am teaching a unit on the Cold War to Year 10, for example, one of my early cumulative tasks is to ask the students to explain why the Cold War emerged, in about one paragraph of writing. Why? Because if they cannot explain in general terms some of the main factors contributing to this, their understanding of later ideas is likely to be distorted. If they are required to do this successfully, they will also need to understand foundational ideas such as Soviet communism, liberal democracy and containment. So a narrative of the emergence of the Cold War and key ideas such as this will be the focus of the teaching and learning that I plan. I now have a clearer idea of what the students should know and remember because I know what they need to do at the end of the process.

Though it may be obvious, it is worth noting that these cumulative tasks for each component are the larger activities that the students will be required to complete at, or towards, the end of the component. They will complete many other activities in each of the lessons throughout the unit, but these will be smaller activities that help the students to consolidate their learning, such as class discussions, brief review quizzes, reading and written response activities, the viewing of video clips and documentaries to develop knowledge of the topic, and more.

Chapter summary

- When you are planning to teach different topics, it helps to know what the major overall task at the end of the unit will be and work towards that overall cumulative goal.
- For each component of the unit, also ensure that students complete a smaller cumulative task that helps them build their knowledge and confidence for the final overall task.
- Ensure that students receive feedback as they move through the components so that they have a better opportunity to demonstrate high-quality work at the end.

End of chapter questions

Questions for reflection and discussion	Questions to ask experienced teachers
1. What is the interplay between the smaller and larger cumulative goals in a topic?	1. How do you build students up towards a large goal within a unit of work such as writing an essay?
2. How do you decide what important knowledge a student needs to know and remember in a topic?	2. How do you know that students have developed deep enough substantive knowledge to complete cumulative tasks?

Further reading

Resource	Why bother reading it?
Dale Banham, "Raising Attainment", in Davies, I. (ed.) *Debates in History Teaching*, London: Routledge, 2017, pp. 215–26	Banham's chapter in *Debates in History Teaching* includes a range of practical tips covering various aspects of secondary history, including reading, research, developing arguments, developing vocabulary and communication. His discussion in this chapter is centred on the question: "How do we develop a culture of excellence?" Part of his answer includes a consideration of how to frame and connect the topics we teach.

CHAPTER 14

Use inquiry questions to guide the whole and the parts

History thrives on curiosity and questions – problems to explore and solve. Why did Rome fall? Why did the industrial revolution break out in European nations first? What was the legacy of the Mongols? Why did the Allies defeat Japan in the Pacific in the Second World War?

In his book *Why Don't Students Like School?*, the psychologist Daniel Willingham argues that, if used intelligently, questions can play an important role in stimulating student interest and directing them towards achievable learning that they may see as valuable. He writes:

> *Sometimes I think that we, as teachers, are so eager to get to the answers that we do not devote sufficient time to developing the question. That probably happens because the answer is obvious to us. But of course it's not obvious to students, and … it's the question that piques people's interest. When you plan a lesson, you start with the information you want students to know by its end. As a next step, consider what the key question for that lesson might be and how you can frame that question so it will have the right level of difficulty to engage your students and so you will respect your students' cognitive limitations.*[49]

As history teachers, we probably have an acute sense of the centrality of questions, since professional historians often pose and respond to major questions of debate and controversy in their work. Questions are a natural feature of the discipline, but this does not mean we are always skilled at posing productive questions for more-novice students, so it needs to be worked at over time.

Questions can also play an important role in making learning aims transparent to students. Instead of simply explaining to students that "today we are going

---

[49] Daniel Willingham, *Why Don't Students Like School? (2nd Ed.)*, Jossey-Bass, 2021, pp. 19-20.

to learn...", we can use questions to keep overarching learning goals clear and to ensure that specific lesson activities are openly connected to a clear sense of overall direction.

Inquiry questions in secondary history

Questions clearly have the potential to help stimulate interest in the material we need to explore, but they can also be powerful tools to give units of work in secondary history and the main components within them what Bob Bain calls "instructional coherence".[50] They can help to bind a sequence of individual lessons together and bring clarity to what the students read, examine, discuss and communicate along the way.

In secondary history, we often use the expression "inquiry question" to refer to an overall problem that students will explore across several lessons and sometimes even an entire topic. It is important to note at the outset, however, that by using the term "inquiry" we are not necessarily referring to something like discovery learning in which students work free of any teacher guidance (see Chapter 4).

TABLE 14.1: Different scales of inquiry question with examples

	Purpose	Examples
Lesson	To provide a clear direction for 1–2 lessons. This question should connect to a sequence-level question.	**Year 7:** What were the main events in the rule of Asoka? **(1 lesson)** **Year 10:** How did the Berlin Airlift contribute to the development of the Cold War? **(1–2 lessons)**
Sequence	To help bind together several lessons (e.g., 4–6) by giving them a common problem to work towards.	**Year 7:** In what ways do the edicts help us understand the rule of Asoka? **(2–3 lessons)** **Year 10:** Why did the US and its allies win the Cold War? **(3–4 lessons)**
Topic	To bring together the learning across an entire topic to help focus the students' attention on key themes and issues within this topic.	**Year 7:** What was the historical significance of the rule of Asoka? **(2–3 focused lessons drawing on the entire unit)** **Year 10:** How did the Cold War shape the 20th century? **(3–4 focused lessons drawing on the entire unit)**

---

50 Robert Bain, "'They Thought the World Was Flat?' Applying the Principles of How People Learn in Teaching High School History", in Donovan, S., and Bransford, J. (eds.) *How Students Learn: History in the Classroom*, National Academies Press, 2005, p. 182.

Planning inquiry questions across an entire unit of work can be a powerful way to organise the teaching and learning activities and bring together meaningful resources that will help students explore and respond to the main questions. These broader topic-level questions might then also become the basis for larger assessment tasks.

Designing and using inquiry questions

There are many ways to begin planning inquiry questions for your units of work. The article by Michael Riley suggested in the further reading section of this chapter is one excellent place to begin. In that, he argues that, at the very least, good inquiry questions should:[51]

- capture the interest and imagination of your students
- place an aspect of historical thinking at the forefront of the students' minds
- result in a tangible, lively, substantial, enjoyable "outcome activity" (i.e., at the end of the lesson sequence) through which students can genuinely answer the enquiry question.

Consider the example in Table 14.1 for a Year 7 unit of work on Asoka the Great: What was the historical significance of the rule of Asoka? This would allow the students to draw on their existing knowledge of Asoka's rule (their substantive knowledge of the topic), require them to grapple with the notion of historical significance (their disciplinary knowledge), and require them to communicate in a sustained manner about both (their practical knowledge).

In my experience, organising a unit of work around inquiry questions can provide a useful snapshot of what a unit will cover and what kinds of activities and resources will be needed. The example provided in Table 14.2 is a unit of work overview for a topic on the late Romanov period of Russian history organised around inquiry questions.

Lesson range

It can also be helpful to avoid strictly limiting the number of individual lessons in which you plan to explore an inquiry question. You will notice in some of the examples already provided that I have suggested a lesson range (e.g., two to three lessons) instead of an exact number. This is because, as Chapter 10 set out, overly rigid planning in the context of secondary education can be dangerous. Given the natural unpredictability of school life, it can be more

---

51 Michael Riley, "Into the Key Stage 3 History Garden: Choosing and Planting Your Enquiry Questions", *Teaching History*, Issue 99, May 2000, pp. 8–13.

helpful to plan slightly flexible sequences of lessons to cover an inquiry question so that they can be scaled up or down as needed.

TABLE 14.2: A unit of work on the decline of the Romanov Dynasty planned through inquiry questions

Topic-level questions	
• Why did the Romanov dynasty collapse in 1917? • To what extent was Nicholas II responsible for the collapse of the Romanov Dynasty in 1917?	
Component-level questions	
A. Historical context	B. Decline and fall
2 weeks (4–6 lessons)	4 weeks (12–14 lessons)
1. What were the origns of the Russian Empire (**2–3 lessons**) 2. To what degree had the Russian Empire changed between 1613 and 1894? (**3–4 lessons**) • Polical structures • Economy • Culture	1. What major challenges faced the Russian Tsar in 1894? (**1 lesson**) 2. Who was Nicholas II and what do contemporary perspectives reveal about his character and rule? (**2–3 lessons**) 3. What caused the emergence of opposition to the tsarist system? (**1 lesson**) 4. What were the perspectives of various groups opposed to the tsarist system in the early 20th century? (**2–3 lessons**) 5. To what extent is there evidence that Nicholas II was successful in ruling the Russian Empire between 1894 and 1914? (**3–4 lessons**) 6. How significant was the First World War to the collapse of the Romanov Dynasty? (**3–4 lessons**)

Chapter summary

- Questions are a powerful tool for organising learning in secondary history.
- Effective inquiry questions in history should allow students to demonstrate substantive and disciplinary knowledge and their ability to communicate about the past.
- Planning to explore inquiry questions should be clear and organised but not overly prescriptive in regards to the number of lessons they might underpin.

End of chapter questions

Questions for reflection and discussion	Questions to ask experienced teachers
1. What kinds of historical questions do you find most interesting? 2. How can inquiry questions help planning in secondary history? 3. Select one topic or theme that is common (or mandatory) in secondary history in your jurisdiction. Draft some key questions that could be used to guide a unit of work similar to that outlined in Table 14.2.	1. How do you ensure that the major questions you set for students to work on are clear, but challenging? 2. What common mistakes do you think are made in setting questions for students to engage with?

Further reading

Resource	Why bother reading it?
Michael Riley, "Into the Key Stage 3 History Garden: Choosing and Planting Your Enquiry Questions", *Teaching History*, Vol. 99, 2000, pp. 8–13	Michael Riley's article on inquiry questions provides an excellent introduction to some of the considerations required to select and refine effective questions for curriculum planning.
Robert Bain, "'They Thought the World Was Flat?' Applying the Principles of How People Learn in Teaching High School History", in Donovan, S., and Bransford, J. (eds.) *How Students Learn: History in the Classroom*, National Academies Press, 2005, pp. 179–213	Bob Bain provides some reasonable and helpful pointers for turning mandated history content into workable problems for students to solve in secondary schools. His emphasis is on ensuring "instructional coherence" and highlighting some of the ways in which questions can help capture this in secondary history.

CHAPTER 15

Keep major assessments embedded and coherent

Assessment is a fundamental part of teaching and learning. It is not just the "big tasks" that students complete at specific junctures throughout a year, but also the smaller, everyday work teachers and students do together that is embedded throughout lessons and activities.[52]

Larger tasks do, however, play an important role in teaching. Not only do schools usually require that students complete large formal assessments during their study, but they can also be powerful tools for synthesising student learning and effort. In secondary history, they can, for example, bring together key substantive, disciplinary and practical knowledge and give the students important opportunities to apply the ideas and principles that have underpinned their learning across longer periods.[53]

Planning for larger assessment tasks

Planning for larger assessment tasks in secondary history should take place while you (perhaps in collaboration with colleagues) plan the general path through a year level or stage. Like many aspects of secondary history, this benefits from macro planning that sits major assessments alongside topic selections. Not only does this allow you to ensure that major tasks are varied, but it also helps you plan your approach to the topics you teach.

Chapter 13 argued, for example, that working towards larger cumulative goals helps to shape the smaller activities that students might complete across a topic and its key parts. Students working towards producing a longer essay at

---

52 Dylan Wiliam and Siobhan Leahy, *Embedding Formative Assessment: Practical Techniques for K–12 Classrooms*, Learning Sciences International, 2015.
53 Denis Schemilt, "Assessment of Learning in History Education: Past, Present, and Possible Futures", in Metzger, S., and Harris, L. (eds.) *The Wiley International Handbook of History Teaching and Learning*, John Wiley and Sons, 2018, pp. 449–71.

the end of the topic as a major assessment should be given many opportunities to examine and draft the key components of an essay to ensure that they are familiar with important conventions and have the opportunity to develop a more confident sense of what quality historical writing might look like in that mode. If the major assessment at the end of another topic is a source-based examination task, then this would shape the activities in different ways again.

Crucially, bringing together *what* students will learn and the ways in which they will be required to communicate their learning means that their efforts form a more natural synthesis and a transparent vision of where they are heading can be developed. It can also ensure that students are given the opportunity to consolidate crucial knowledge and skills across major tasks without repeating the same narrow assessments in every year.

Table 15.1 sets out one possible macro plan for major assessments, assuming that students will complete two major tasks in each year level that they study history across Years 7–10. Note that students have multiple opportunities to engage with similar tasks, even though there is variety across the four years of their engagement with history. It is also realistic in pointing out that assessment choices are not always made by the teacher. Sometimes, for example, schools impose policies where year groups must complete a major examination across all core subjects at the end of a year.

TABLE 15.1: One possible major assessment plan for Years 7–10

Year 7	**Task 1:** Written responses about a major case study from the ancient world including source-based questions
	Task 2: Individual presentation on a chosen aspect of the case studies completed in class throughout the year (the list includes people, groups, sites and objects)
Year 8	**Task 1:** Source-based written task completed in class
	Task 2: Small-group presentation on a theme/question selected from a list provided by the teacher or created by the students and cleared with the teacher
Year 9	**Task 1:** Essay response selected from a small list of questions provided by the teacher
	Task 2: End-of-year examination including source-based questions (examinations in this context are a whole-school requirement)
Year 10	**Task 1:** Essay incorporating primary sources
	Task 2: End-of-year examination including source-based questions (examinations in this context are a whole-school requirement)

The assessment should not be decoding the task

In my early years of teaching I recall setting a task for a group of students in Year 7 in which I created a formal assessment notification that included ludicrous detail in terms of the directions students had to follow. There was a list of topics that students could select from, several clauses outlining the major components of the sub-tasks within the broader task, checklists and marking criteria that, collectively, amounted to several pages. When I found the task a few years later, I was utterly embarrassed that I had produced such an overwhelming document. It had, however, taught me a valuable lesson: that if the students need to spend more time understanding the task than completing it – an obvious, but useful exaggeration – something has gone wrong.

Provide a clear and succinct notification

When I now work with teachers and model the process of putting together a formal notification for a major assessment task in secondary history, I try to stress that it is important to strike a balance between providing clear directions on the one hand and keeping the notification succinct on the other. Teachers should, I suggest, think hard about the essential details that need to be included in setting out the requirements of a major assessment.

As a basic rule, I aim to keep major assessment notifications to about two A4 pages, particularly for Years 7–10. On this, I try to include:

- A brief overview of the task
- Crucial information such as due dates (and times if required) and submission instructions
- Some specific directions outlining the main task requirements
- A marking rubric identifying three or four main areas that will form the basis of my observations and feedback
- Links to any formal policy documents that the students might require, such as a faculty referencing guide or school assessment policy regarding late submissions.

It is also crucial that all key requirements of a major assessment are transparently communicated. For example, if the students are required to write an essay and incorporate evidence from primary sources, it is only fair to state up front how many sources they are expected to include. It is unfair to leave this open-ended and then, in the process of marking the students' work, punish some for not including enough. Instead of saying "You will be required to refer to primary sources in your response", therefore, in most cases I would opt for a more specific direction such as "Your response should incorporate evidence from two or three primary sources". If, in the latter example, a student refers to none or only one, I have every right to argue that their use of primary sources was insufficient.

Clear and powerful questions

In tasks that require students to respond to a specific question (or select one from a list of alternatives), I try to ensure that these are succinctly worded and easy to comprehend but still open up powerful opportunities for students who are more confident.

For example, consider the following questions:

A. What were the most important motivations for Spanish imperial expansion in the 15th and 16th centuries? What role did religion, economics and other factors play in creating the Spanish empire?
B. Account for the expansion of the Spanish empire in the 15th and 16th centuries.

Both questions essentially aim to have the students analyse and argue about the same issue: the factors underpinning Spain's expansion in the 15th and 16th centuries. The first version of the question, however, is double-barrelled in that it poses a question and then adds another more specific question on top. The second part of that question could be eliminated and used in additional task directions if deemed essential, but it is not required to make the first part of the question valuable.

The second version, by contrast, is shorter and sharper. If the students have worked on a topic exploring the Spanish empire, it should take little time for them to understand what the question asks of them. In addition, the question allows students who might find this task harder to demonstrate what they know and can do – they might only write or speak about two factors underpinning Spanish expansion. More-confident students can respond to this question with a complex evaluative argument demonstrating a richer understanding of historical causation and historical interpretations such as the following: "Although some historians stress the religious motivations for the expansion of the Spanish empire in the 15th century, the most important factors explaining this phenomenon were ultimately economic". This question allows the less confident student to communicate their understanding, but, crucially, it does not limit the more confident student from putting forward more complex ideas and so demonstrating their knowledge and abilities.

Scaffolds and templates

In many tasks, I also try to scaffold and provide templates that help to focus students' attention on key aspects of the task. If it is a research task, for example, and the students are required to produce a bibliography of the resources they used to complete the assessment, I give them a template for a bibliography so that they do not waste time trying to figure out what a well-structured bibliography looks like – the important point for them is to do the research, not create a new design for a bibliography.

In class presentations requiring students to stand up and speak, I often impose clear boundaries on what is required in terms of supporting material. If I want students to present historical arguments verbally with the use of PowerPoint slides or something similar, I might impose the following restrictions:

- You are limited to a maximum of six slides.
- One slide must include your question clearly visible and your overall thesis statement.
- The only other words allowed are shorter extracts from primary or secondary sources and basic labels and/or headings where required.

This can help model better use of tools such as PowerPoint, forcing the students away from text-heavy slides and towards actively using these to bring their argument to life by speaking to maps, images or diagrams or evaluating and discussing historical sources as they communicate their ideas. It can also help to keep the students' attention focused on the most important thinking and communicating that the task requires (making and justifying an argument) rather than spending inordinate amounts of time designing PowerPoint slides.

In addition, scaffolding can be embedded across entire topics as students move towards major assessments. For example, if the students are required to develop a written argument in essay form, they might be given many opportunities to build and evaluate arguments in other forms throughout a topic, specifically targeting key argumentative terms (such as conclusion and premise), crafting clear thesis statements, effective use of evidence, and other key practical requirements.

Student choice

Embedding elements of student choice in major assessments can be a powerful way to keep history open, ensure that there are opportunities for students to lean into areas of the subject that they find more interesting, and maintain variety in your classes.

This does, however, need to be used carefully to ensure that major assessments, particularly if they are formal tasks that count towards external grading, remain balanced and equitable. To assist this, you might:

- Provide a list of options that students can select from to ensure that the questions or topics are even in their requirements
- Include the possibility of proposing a completely different question/topic provided that it is cleared with you as the teacher first. This way you can ensure that the students select something appropriate and reasonable.

In some contexts, it can also be entirely appropriate to open up student choice even further to what I called "guided independence" in Chapter 4. Here students might be given considerable freedom to select topics, refine questions, and propose different mediums for communicating their ideas.

Chapter summary

- Major assessments are a key part of secondary history.
- Macro planning is an important way to ensure that major assessments meet school policy requirements and that students are granted various opportunities to demonstrate their abilities in history.
- Larger formal assessments usually require task notifications that clearly and succinctly communicate the key requirements of a task.
- Student choice can be a powerful dimension of larger tasks, but this may be provided with particular boundaries to ensure that tasks remain equitable and clear.

End of chapter questions

Questions for reflection and discussion	Questions to ask experienced teachers
1. What kinds of major assessments do you recall completing in secondary history when you were are school? 2. Do you recall completing any tasks that you enjoyed more/less? Describe them. 3. How can formal assessment task notifications balance the need for clarity and succinctness?	1. How do you plan out your major assessments across year levels? 2. What rules and procedures does your school have for major assessment tasks?

Further reading

Resource	Why bother reading it?
Bruce VanSledgright, "Assessing for Learning in the History Classroom", in Ercikan, K., and Seixas, P. (2015) *New Directions in Assessing Historical Thinking*, Routledge, 2015, pp. 75–88	VanSledgright's discussion in this chapter offers some useful ideas about assessing students' historical thinking in secondary contexts.
Denis Schemilt, "Assessment of Learning in History Education: Past, Present, and Possible Futures", in Metzger, S., and Harris, L. (eds.) *The Wiley International Handbook of History Teaching and Learning*, John Wiley and Sons, 2018, pp. 449–71	Schemilt discusses a range of important ideas relating to assessment in history. His analysis discusses the purposes of assessment as well as different modes of assessment that might be employed in secondary history.
Jonathon Dallimore, "The Three Move Thesis: Explicitly Teaching Students to Develop Logical Arguments", *Teaching History*, Vol. 55, No. 4, 2021, pp. 11–13	This article outlines some strategies for teaching students to construct logical arguments. It outlines key terminology, key concepts and tips for implementation that can be adapted for a variety of topics and age ranges in secondary history.

Part Three
Sequences and Lessons

CHAPTER 16

Work on developing content, complexity and communication

After you have broken down the topic you will be teaching into its main component parts and decided which of those you will spend more and less time on, you then need to start organising the teaching activities and the resources that go with them so that students have a way of working through each area.

Developing units of work is likely to be the result of an interplay between the questions and themes you want to explore with the students and what resources you have access to or can create in a reasonable timeframe. Sometimes you will develop an inquiry question and then find or create the resources to work through it. At other times, you will find existing resources and develop a sequence of lessons around them because they are high-quality and fit within your overarching aims for the unit. Often, planning units of work will involve a combination of both, sometimes leaning more on the former and at other times leaning more on the latter.

A simple start

As you begin thinking about how you might work through each of the components of the topic you are teaching and what resources might be needed for each section, a simple but broadly useful process to consider is planning the teaching and learning around content, complexity and communication.

Content

The term "content" here refers essentially to substantive knowledge. Students need to develop a sense of the story relevant to the topic. They need to know facts and information about the topic that are useful to the inquiry they are exploring; otherwise they are likely to have little to say at the end.

As students begin exploring a topic, it is likely that a broad overview will be a good place to start – for example, watching a documentary or short film about the topic to develop a broad sense of the key narrative, themes, individuals and groups. This could easily be supplemented by closely examining a timeline or reading from a textbook, website or other ready-made resource.

Complexity

The term "complexity" here essentially refers to disciplinary knowledge. To develop a truly rich understanding of the inquiry they are pursuing, students are likely to need to explore this through some more detailed and complex ideas.

As the students' general understanding of the topic grows, there should be opportunity to introduce more complex concepts and material. These might include specific engagement with disciplinary concepts (such as causation and change and continuity), more detailed source material (such as primary documents), or the different interpretations of historians.

Communication

As has been stated already in this book, it is impossible to be sure of what students know about the topic you are studying unless they communicate in some form. Communication should, therefore, be a constant feature of every topic, though communication can include many forms.

Communication can be as simple as students responding to quiz questions or participating in a more impromptu class discussion. It could, and at some point should, also involve communicating in more substantial forms such as extended writing tasks that draw together their knowledge of the topic they are studying and allow them to apply their knowledge and understanding.

A basic example

One simple example of employing this "content, complexity, communication" approach might be the following. Imagine that you are beginning to teach a five-to-six-lesson sequence exploring the experience of Allied prisoners of war in the Pacific during the Second World War. Our overarching inquiry question might be: "Why did the perspectives of Allied prisoners of war in the Pacific during the Second World War vary so much?" If we were moving through the content, complexity and communication stages in a completely linear manner, the five-to-six-lesson sequence might look like that outlined in Table 16.1.

TABLE 16.1: A possible lesson sequence investigating the experiences of Allied prisoners of war in the Pacific during the Second World War

Lesson no. and focus	Basic summary	Key resource(s)
Lesson 1: Content	The first lesson introduces the main inquiry question and then aims to provide students with a broad overview of the experience of Allied prisoners of war in the Pacific during the Second World War. The main (not the only) activity will be watching a documentary about prisoners in the Pacific and taking notes that respond to guided questions on the topic.	Documentary and guided questions
Lesson 2: Content	To consolidate their use of the documentary in lesson 1, in this second lesson, students will read a one-or-two-page extract from a textbook (or similar source) that provides another overview of the main theme in the enquiry. Students read the text, respond to some questions in their workbooks or on their devices, and then discuss their answers together as a class.	Textbook reading and questions
Lesson 3: Complexity	By this stage students should be aware of the general story of captivity in the Pacific during the Second World War and should be able to describe and explain key features of this experience. In this lesson they might begin exploring these experiences using several primary sources from survivors who left diaries, letters, interviews and memoirs.	A small collection of curated sources to be explored in pairs or small groups.
Lesson 4: Complexity/ communication	In this lesson the students finalise their exploration of the prisoners' experience with the sources they began to explore in the previous lesson. They then begin to plan to write a paragraph responding to the main inquiry question in the following lesson through some teacher-directed planning using a scaffold.	The same sources as the previous lesson and one writing scaffold for the main communication task.

Lesson no. and focus	Basic summary	Key resource(s)
Lesson 5: Communication	In the final lesson of this sequence, the students revise common requirements for constructing formal written responses in history (including referring explicitly to source material). They then write their responses and submit these to the teacher for formal feedback.	A printed handout providing space for the students to write a response to the main enquiry question that can be submitted to the teacher for feedback. Obviously, this could also be done digitally on devices such as laptops if that opportunity exists.

In the example set out in Table 16.1, the class would be first concentrating on developing content, followed by exploring that content in more complexity and then synthesising and communicating their understanding in substantial form at the end.

A more realistic example

This pattern of content, complexity and communication is another useful tool that should not be treated rigidly. The simple example set out in Table 16.1 is neat, but the reality is likely to be messier, even though the focus may remain on content, complexity and communication. Consider a slightly adjusted alternative to the original sequence in table 16.2. This alternative would essentially make use of the same activities and resources, but in this version, we can hopefully see many more layers to each lesson and to the sequence as a whole.

TABLE 16.2: A possible lesson sequence investigating the experiences of Allied prisoners of war in the Pacific during the Second World War

	Lesson 1	Lesson 2	Lesson 3	Lesson 4	Lesson 5
Content	Viewing a documentary, taking notes and pausing to discuss.	Textbook reading and guided questions.	Reviewed at the beginning of the lesson with a short quiz.	Reviewed at the beginning of the lesson with verbal questions.	Used by students to construct their written paragraphs.

	Lesson 1	Lesson 2	Lesson 3	Lesson 4	Lesson 5
Complexity	Introduce the enquiry by examining two primary source photographs.	Reading introduces more complex detail.	Primary sources from prisoners held captive in different regions of the Pacific.	Primary source investigation continued from the previous lesson.	Used by students to construct their written paragraphs.
Communication	Simple verbal review questions asked by the teacher.	Written responses to guided reading questions and class discussion.	Small group reporting to the whole class guided by the teacher.	Conventions of formal writing revised and modelled.	Students write paragraphs to submit for teacher review.

This second example provides a more realistic impression of how many effective history sequences operate. It is less obviously linear in that content, complexity and communication feature in some manner in most, if not all, of the five lessons in the sequence. Importantly, however, it still demonstrates that content, complexity and communication are useful ways to ensure that the learning in a sequence of lessons is robust and that student effort comes together in a useful cumulative activity.

Checking for gaps

If you arrive at the end of a sequence of lessons such as those outlined in Tables 16.1 and 16.2 and the students attempt to produce a substantial piece of writing but only produce shallow responses that lack detail, one question to consider is whether the sequence included enough attention to content and complexity. It may be that this was insufficiently addressed during the lessons and so the students, assuming they made a genuine effort in the writing task, may simply not have known enough to produce written work of higher quality. Other factors may have been at play too, but reflecting on how much time for content and complexity was allocated across the lessons could help to improve your teaching of this sequence in the future.

Chapter summary

- One way to begin organising the teaching and learning activities for a sequence of lessons is to consider when and how you might focus on content, complexity and communication.

- These are not likely to be embedded linearly across every sequence of lessons, but they should consistently be explored if students are to develop a deeper understanding of the topics they are required to explore.
- There are many creative ways of adapting this idea, and like many other aspects of this book, the suggestion to consider content, complexity and communication should only be a starting point, not a prescriptive rule to be followed uniformly at every point in your teaching.

End of chapter questions

Questions for reflection and discussion	Questions to ask experienced teachers
1. What is meant by the terms content, complexity and communication? 2. Explain why this approach is not necessarily a linear approach always starting with content and moving through to complexity. 3. Why is it important to ensure that students are regularly communicating about the topic you are studying with them?	1. What activities do you use to get students communicating about their work other than read and response or discussions? 2. How do you ensure that students have developed a strong enough understanding of a topic before you get them to communicate in extended form such as writing?

Further reading

Resource	Why bother reading it?
Dale Banham, "Raising Attainment", in Davies, I. (ed.) *Debates in History Teaching*, Routledge, 2017, pp. 215–26	Banham's chapter in *Debates in History Teaching* includes a range of practical tips covering various aspects of secondary history, including reading, research, developing arguments, developing vocabulary and communication. His discussion in this chapter is centred on the question: "How do we develop a culture of excellence?" Part of his answer includes a consideration of how to frame and connect the topics we teach.

CHAPTER 17

Aim to challenge and support every student

Planning to appropriately challenge all students is a key component of teaching secondary history. In almost all teaching contexts we will be working with students of mixed ability, including those who already excel in the subject, those who have made very little progress in their learning so far, and all points in between. It is no good in these contexts to plan topics that cater to the needs of one small group but leave the other students to flounder or be held back by limited aspirations.

In discussing the challenge of teaching classes that include students with a range of achievement levels, the history teacher Bruce Lesh helpfully explains that instead of taking a unit of work and cutting out the parts that some students might find most difficult (that is, reducing the demands of the unit), he instead attempts to plan to include teaching and resources that will help support all students to make progress in those challenging areas.[54] The overall expectations remain high yet reasonable, but additional support is embedded into the teaching plan to assist those students who need it most. This concept of teaching with appropriate aspiration underpins the considerations in this chapter.

Expectations

In a now-famous study conducted in the mid-1960s with primary school teachers and students in the United States, Robert Rosenthal and Lenore Jacobson suggested that "one person's expectations of another's behaviour may come to serve as a self-fulfilling prophecy".[55] In essence, they

---

54 Bruce Lesh, *Developing Historical Thinkers: Supporting Historical Inquiry for All Learners*, Teachers College Press, 2023, pp. 27–28.
55 Robert Rosenthal and Lenore Jacobson, "Pygmalion in the Classroom", *The Urban Review*, Vol. 3, 1968, p. 20.

demonstrated that individual students made more observable progress when their teachers held high expectations of them. Studies have since continued to explore and affirm the general notion that high expectations in supportive environments are crucial to student success in schools.[56]

In more practical terms, holding high expectations of the students that you teach in secondary history includes:

- Believing that all students can make progress towards higher achievement
- Planning topics, assessments and lessons that aim to raise student achievement
- Communicating high expectations to all students in a supportive manner
- Holding the students to high standards in behaviour, activities, class discussions, tasks and feedback.

It should be noted that high expectations are for the long term. That is, we may not expect students to immediately master the knowledge and skills required, but, over time, with careful teaching, effort, clear guidance, opportunities to practise, and helpful feedback, all students can improve. In that sense, it can require considerable patience on a teacher's part, since many students genuinely do find aspects of history difficult.

Though high expectations can be challenging, the alternative is bleak. Instead of holding appropriate aspirations for the students we teach, we would be expecting failure, dumbing down class work to make it easier, and essentially guaranteeing that student progress could only be made in spite of our efforts.

Teaching to the top

When discussing strategies for teaching classes of mixed-attainment students, it is now popular to talk about "teaching to the top". This can be a useful term provided we avoid thinking that it refers to the "top of the class" and not to the "top standards". In other words, teaching to the top directs a whole class's attention to the highest demands of the curriculum, not the handful of students who are already there.

In *Teaching to the Top: Aiming High for Every Learner* (2021), Megan Mansworth argues that:

> ... *the vision for teaching to the top I emphasise in this book is one of consistently teaching higher-level ideas and knowledge and making this*

---

56 Megan Mansworth, *Teaching to the Top: Aiming High for Every Learner*, John Catt, 2021, pp. 31–32.

accessible to all students in our classes ... ensuring that every student is afforded access to the most stimulating, challenging and thought-provoking learning opportunities.[57]

Note that, in her definition, Mansworth is stressing the quality of ideas and activities that students spend their time on. In a plan to teach to the top, the central question is: "In the context of this age and topic, what high-quality substantive, disciplinary and practical knowledge should we aim to master?"

To take one concrete example, if our curriculum for Year 10 history requires students to "explain key factors leading to the outbreak of the First World War in 1914", this should become the minimum aim for all students in the class that we are teaching. If we know that some may find it difficult and will need time to be able to explain how a range of causal factors contributed to the outbreak of that conflict, we should consider finding ways to teach towards that goal rather than abandoning it for something simpler.

At the same time, there is no reason that in this context we may not also provide some opportunities to extend those students who are likely to reach this goal more quickly. They might, for example, reach this minimum goal and then be set free to explore and evaluate some of those causal factors or even begin investigating key historical interpretations of the outbreak of the First World War and thus remain challenged. The important point is that demonstrating an ability to "explain the key factors leading to the outbreak of the First World War in 1914" has become the baseline expectation for all students, not the limiting expectation.

In Diagram 17.1 (overleaf) this scenario is outlined in more detail. If the baseline expectation is that students need to explain factors (that is more than one) that contributed to the outbreak of the First World War, at some point we need all students to attempt this. Though we might begin by requiring students to work below this baseline expectation to build up their knowledge and confidence – by addressing tasks (i) and (ii) in the diagram – if that is the extent of their learning, we are limiting expectations to below the baseline, which is teaching towards the bottom rather than the top. At same point, we would need to look for an opportunity for students to attempt at least task (a). Those who can quickly and confidently achieve task (a) might be then given freedom to extend further and complete task (b). The direction of travel for all students is up.

---

57 Megan Mansworth, *Teaching to the Top: Aiming High for Every Learner*, John Catt, 2021, p. 9.

DIAGRAM 17.1: An example of teaching to the top with the outbreak of the First World War

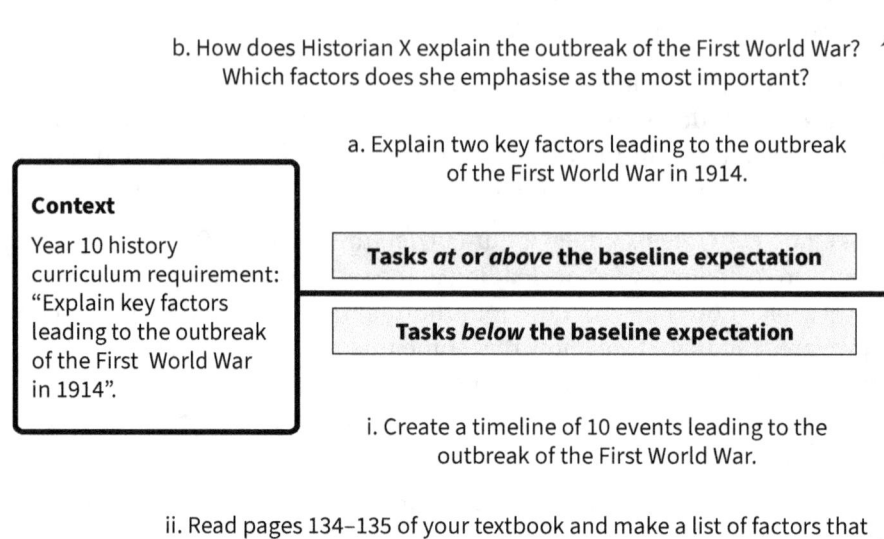

On a larger scale, if we are required to teach essay-writing to a year group, teaching to the top would involve setting the writing of a complete essay as the baseline expectation and teaching towards that goal. We could not substitute that goal with writing a brief description or narrative if they found this challenging. We would try to find ways to support them in achieving the higher goal.

Scaffolding

In planning to teach with high expectations, it is also important to ensure that we plan to provide lots of support to the students who will need it. We have already noted that history is an "unnatural act", and so we should expect that many students will need direct assistance as they try to understand complex concepts, work with historical sources, communicate in technical and extended forms, and so on. If we are to keep those ambitious goals as the baseline targets for all students, we also need to be willing to build students incrementally towards those goals.

In aiming to do this, we will be required to scaffold the teaching of key ideas and skills for students. Even the most able students will often need some assistance as they develop their substantive, disciplinary and practical knowledge in history. Scaffolding has a long and complex history, and there are important debates about its precise meaning.[58] For practical purposes, however, we might best divide it into "build-up" scaffolding and "completion" scaffolding.

TABLE 17.1: Build-up and completion scaffolding

Build-up scaffolding	These activities and strategies aim to incrementally build students up towards more complex ideas and skills. If students are to write an extended argumentative piece, for example, in the weeks leading up to this we might plan to build them up by explicitly addressing technical vocabulary that they might use, modelling key argumentative structures, reviewing examples of high-quality argumentative writing, and more. Each of these activities and strategies should give the students greater confidence to step out on their own in the ultimate task of producing an extended argumentative piece.
Completion scaffolding	These are tools that we might offer students *as* they complete an activity or task to help guide their work. Keeping with the example above, it might include vocabulary lists for optional use on the day that they write their extended argumentative piece. It might also include some sentence starters or a more complete writing template that helps students focus on expressing key ideas.

It is crucial that we aim for scaffolds to be taken away over time. If students endlessly fill in writing frames, always rely on vocabulary lists, and are never required to move beyond these structures, the scaffolds are likely to have become a limitation rather than a platform towards greater confidence and independence.

Chapter summary

- Appropriately high expectations are important for academic success in secondary history.
- High expectations should be embedded in our curriculum, topic and lesson planning.
- Teaching to the top can help to ensure that the focus of all students remains on high-quality ideas and skills.
- Providing encouragement and support through scaffolding and other teaching strategies is a crucial dimension of teaching to the top.

---

58 Anna Shvarts and Arthur Bakker, "The Early History of the Scaffolding Metaphor: Bernstein, Luria, Vygotsky and Before", *Mind, Culture and Activity*, Vol. 26, No. 1, 2019, pp. 4–23.

End of chapter questions

Questions for reflection and discussion	Questions to ask experienced teachers
1. Why are appropriately high expectations important for teaching? 2. How do teacher beliefs form an important part of high expectations? 3. What is generally meant by the term "teaching to the top"? 4. Re-examine Diagram 17.1 and create your own similar visual for another topic or theme that you are required to teach. 5. What is the aim of scaffolding? 6. List some different scaffolding strategies for "build-up" and "completion".	1. How do you challenge all students in classes where attainment levels vary widely? 2. What specific strategies do you use to support students who find history more difficult? 3. How do you ensure that students who are more confident are provided with opportunities to excel?

Further reading

Resource	Why bother reading it?
Megan Mansworth, *Teaching to the Top: Aiming High for Every Learner*, John Catt Educational, 2021	Mansworth's book *Teaching to the Top* is not written by or for history teachers, but it is clear and practical. It sets out some helpful thinking about the concept of teaching to the top, with practical advice, even though it is not specific to the subject of history.
Rachel Ball, "Scaffolding in History" in Fairlamb, A., and Ball, R. (eds.) *What Is History Teaching Now? A Practical Handbook for All History Teachers and Educators*, John Catt, 2023	This brief chapter offers some additional discussion of specific approaches to scaffolding in history subjects. In contrast to many other books covering generic ideas about scaffolding, this specifically relates to history teaching, so all examples provided are concretely relevant.
Chris Runeckles, *Making Every History Lesson Count: Six Principles to Support Great History Teaching*, Crown House Publishing, 2018 (Chapter 1: "Challenge")	Chris Runeckles sets out some practical advice for ensuring that expectations are met in secondary history without unnecessarily burdening students in the process.

Resource	Why bother reading it?
Kay Traille, *Hearing Their Voices: Teaching History to Students of Color*, Rowman and Littlefield, 2019	Traille's research provides important insights into the considerations that history teachers need to prioritise when teaching diverse students. This also includes ideas for supporting marginalised students in secondary history.

CHAPTER 18

Anticipate errors and misconceptions

Most veteran teachers of secondary school subjects could name a suite of common errors and misconceptions they regularly encounter. These could be procedural errors in solving mathematical equations, conceptual misunderstanding in English, poor technique in music, and more.

History also has its share of common errors and misconceptions. This should not be a surprise, however, since students arrive at secondary history classes with many preconceived ideas about certain topics and about the past itself. These are often the residue of students' exposure to popular culture, such as films, memes and music, and also their exposure to public memory about history, which may vary widely in the quality of ideas it encourages.[59]

Perhaps most legendary among the common errors and misconceptions in history are, however, those associated with historical sources. These include claims such as:

- "This source is not useful because it is biased" (as though partisan sources can never reveal anything of value to a historian)
- "Primary sources are more useful than secondary sources" (as though historians with access to far more knowledge cannot present more insightful accounts of the past because they were "not there at the time")
- "The letter is from an American perspective" (as though one letter could speak for all Americans).

When approaching lessons in secondary history, as in any subject, it is worth considering what common errors and misconceptions may arise and, where possible, planning to head these off before they become too great a problem.

---

59 Peter Lee and Denis Schemilt, "'I Just Wish We Could Go Back in the Past and Find Out What Really Happened: Progression in Understanding about Historical Accounts", *Teaching History*, Vol. 117, 2004, p. 26.

This can be challenging, however, and some errors and misconceptions can be extremely stubborn.

Errors of substance

The most basic errors that students can make in secondary history are probably factual inaccuracies. Associating reforms with the wrong monarch or government, mixing up dates or chronology, and using incorrect technical terms to describe groups or events are all common examples of inaccuracies that easily creep into history.

These are entirely normal, particularly when students are new to a topic and learning complex material for the first time. They might be learning about a new geographic region, coming to terms with a new chronology, grappling with new concepts such as democracy, imperialism or communism, or learning the names of key individuals and groups for the first time. In these circumstances, it would be surprising if mistakes were not common.

It can be extremely difficult to predict what factual inaccuracies might emerge with any particular class or topic, so it can be hard to fight these before they appear. This only stresses the importance, then, of regularly checking in on students' substantive knowledge of the topics that you are exploring through formative assessment.

These ideas will be explored further in Chapter 23, but it is important here to stress that students should be given a range of opportunities to revisit and consolidate their understanding of those aspects of substantive knowledge that they *must* know to thrive in the topic you are exploring. It would be difficult, for example, for students studying the Roman Republic to make much progress without a secure and accurate knowledge of concepts such as senate, consul, patrician and plebeian. If students were constantly mixing up the patricians and plebeians, we would expect their ideas communicated in discussions or writing to be of limited quality. So, in the context of this topic, concepts such as these would deserve specific attention. They might be explored through several resources and targeted in quizzes and class discussions to ensure that any misconceptions are eliminated as quickly as possible.

Disciplinary misconceptions and oversimplifications

Students also often develop misconceptions relating to disciplinary aspects of secondary history. Often these involve misconceptions revealing a superficial understanding of key ideas that historians rely on.

Common examples of this include the simplistic and erroneous ideas about historical sources outlined at the beginning of this chapter. We might also include misconceptions or oversimplifications relating to key disciplinary ideas such as causation or change and continuity.

When exploring these crucial disciplinary concepts and skills, then, it is important that students are given useful models and directions to apply as they develop their thinking. This can include scaffolds that force their thinking away from simplistic ideas and towards richer conceptualisations of the past.

If, for example, I am getting a group of Year 10 students to think more deeply about causation, I might require them to specifically identify and explore a range of different causal factors that help to explain some aspect of the past. I might do this through guided questions or, alternatively, I might use a visual scaffold that helps the students track and share their thinking. This might require students to specifically consider longer- and shorter-term causes or different kinds of historical causes such as economic, political, social/cultural and individuals/groups. My essential aim in doing this is to ensure that students begin shaping multi-causal arguments that move beyond shallow explanations.

DIAGRAM 18.1: Common causal explanations in history

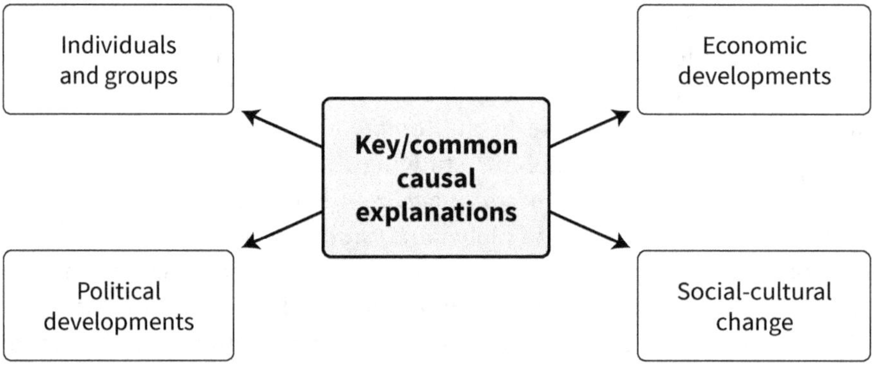

```
    Individuals                          Economic
    and groups                         developments
            ↘                         ↗
              Key/common
                causal
              explanations
            ↗                         ↘
    Political                         Social-cultural
   developments                          change
```

When exploring issues of change and continuity, it is not uncommon for students to focus almost entirely on change and ignore important continuities and vice versa. In attempts to prevent this, I often try to create activities that force the students to think about how change and continuity may have both been evident during the period we are exploring. If, for example, we are studying a political movement such as a dictatorship, our main goal might be to question how revolutionary the regime was during the leadership of a particular individual or group. Instead of getting the students to generally consider change and continuity, I might require them to track these concepts across different areas of society and demonstrate their thinking visually, as in diagram 18.2. This particular example would suggest that the student considers the regime to have been more revolutionary in the political and economic spheres than in the social and cultural spheres.

DIAGRAM 18.2: Tracking change and continuity

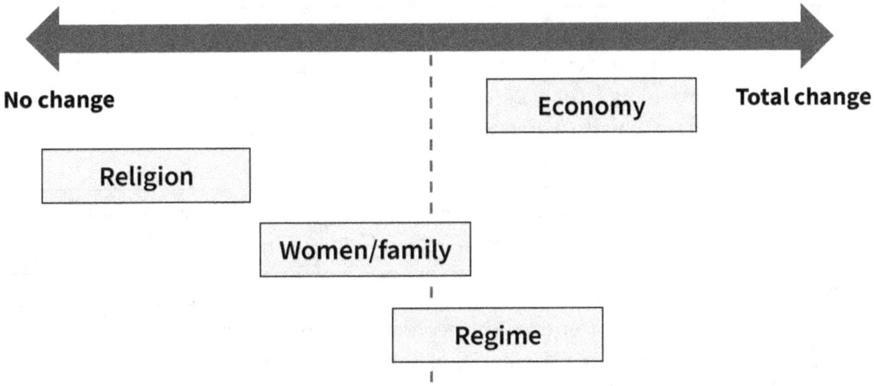

No change ←――――――――――――――――――→ Total change

- Religion
- Women/family
- Regime
- Economy

Practical errors

Students also often make significant errors when completing more practical work in history such as writing short responses or longer essays. Again, some of the common errors are well-known, including:

- Forgetting to include a clear thesis statement in the introduction to an essay
- Creating paragraphs that are far too long or short in essays
- Leaving out key references to required sources in responses
- Slipping into narrative or descriptive writing modes when it is necessary to argue and analyse.

As with disciplinary misconceptions and oversimplifications, these practical errors can take time to weed out. When it comes to writing in particular – a core part of secondary history – these problems often require repeated and consistent effort on the part of the teacher and student. Table 18.1 (overleaf) outlines some basic approaches to embed within planning that will help guide students towards improvement in these areas.

TABLE 18.1: Anticipating common errors in historical writing

Providing samples	Providing students with clear and strong samples of the kind of writing you want them to produce will help clarify key conventions and expectations.
Modelling	Sometimes, actively creating written text with the class in real time can help students see and hear the thought processes that go into strong historical writing. Doing this in real time can provide added opportunities to ask probing questions of the class and revisit ideas that have already been explored.
Planning and drafting	Providing students with opportunities to plan and draft before they commit to detailed and extended writing can also help prevent problems arising. Before writing a complete essay, for example, require them to write a draft thesis statement in response to the question and discuss its strengths and weaknesses.
Practice	Students need multiple opportunities to practise the various kinds of writing that are common in your jurisdiction.
Feedback	Regular feedback is crucial to students' consolidation of strong habits in historical writing. This feedback could be verbal, written, whole class, individual or a combination. It should also require the students to think actively about their work and plan for future opportunities to practise and improve.

Chapter summary

- Common errors and misconceptions are a feature of all secondary subjects.
- Common errors and misconceptions in secondary history can relate to the substantive, disciplinary and practical aspects of the subject.
- Planning to help students avoid these errors is an important aspect of teaching secondary history.

End of chapter questions

Questions for reflection and discussion	Questions to ask experienced teachers
1. What does it mean to anticipate challenges in secondary history? 2. Review some of the common substantive, disciplinary and practical errors outlined in this chapter. Are there others that you have seen or are aware of? Describe them. 3. How do scaffolds and other tools help to avoid common errors in secondary history?	1. What common errors do you see students making in secondary history? 2. What kinds of scaffolds do you often use in secondary history?

Further reading

Resource	Why bother reading it?
Bruce VanSledgright, "Assessing for Learning in the History Classroom", in Ercikan, K., and Seixas, P. (2015) *New Directions in Assessing Historical Thinking*, Routledge, 2015, pp. 75–88	VanSledgright's discussion in this chapter offers some useful ideas about assessing students' historical thinking in secondary contexts.
Tom Sherrington, *Rosenshine's Principles in Action*, John Catt Educational Ltd, 2019	This short book includes a useful exposition of some key findings from the research of Barack Rosenshine. It includes helpful tips for checking students' understanding and providing opportunities for student practice.
James Durran, "Modelling and How to Plan for It", 13 August 2024: https://jamesdurran.blog/2024/08/13/modelling-and-how-to-plan-for-it/	James Durran provides a clear and useful overview of some key ideas relating to modelling. He helpfully examines some different approaches to modelling and also explores some common hazards with modelling. There are many useful diagrams and visuals that accompany the post.

CHAPTER 19

Use historical sources meaningfully

In many ways, historical sources have come to be the air that history teachers breathe. As far back as 1913 Maurice Keatinge argued in his discussion of teaching secondary history that: "our pupils must be confronted with [historical] documents, and forced to exercise their minds upon them".[60] Modern textbooks are often crammed with images, extracts and graphic reconstructions. Institutions such as libraries and museums make source collections available online too. The rapid expansion of cheap, high-speed internet in the early 2000s only encouraged the prevalence of sources, which, on the whole, is positive.

One of the dangers with the proliferation of sources, however, is that we risk losing a mindful approach to using them; we run the risk of just assuming that working with sources is useful and "right" or that studying history is *just* critically examining sources. But that is not always the case, and we would do well to ensure that we use sources in meaningful ways in the classroom as much as possible.

I would argue that meaningful work with sources in secondary history should be grounded in balance, consistency and an incremental increase in the complexity of what students are expected to do with this material. In terms of balance, Peter Lee has perceptively argued that:

> *It would be absurd to insist that pupils test everything they are taught by direct recourse to the relevant sources, let alone produce all their history from the sources themselves. It is equally absurd, however, to say that schoolchildren know any history if they have no understanding of how historical knowledge is attained, its relationship to evidence, and the*

---

60 Maurice Keatinge, *Studies in the Teaching of History*, Adam and Charles Black, 1913, p. 38.

> way in which historians arbitrate between competing or contradictory claims.⁶¹

In terms of consistency and incremental challenge, Stéphane Lévesque warns that:

> ... unless students are exposed gradually and persistently to the practice of investigating the past using sources, sporadic attempts (for a lesson or two) seem to have limited impact on their historical learning. "Teaching children to think historical", VanSledright concludes, "is a slow, arduous process. The more novice the student, the more time and intensive energy it takes".⁶²

This tension between avoiding an overemphasis on sources as the foundation for everything in secondary history and a consistent approach lies at the heart of this chapter.

Taking stock

To the untrained eye, work with sources in secondary history often just looks like repetitive "source analysis" activity – usually with the implied meaning that this is simply a mechanical process with little or no connection to the students' broader learning.

While this may occur, many history teachers actively use sources for a purpose and these are, more often than not, likely to relate to common strategies that have been outlined in teaching advice for many decades. In 1972, for example, A. D. Edwards argued in his chapter in the second edition of *Handbook for History Teachers* that there are at least four intelligent and common uses of sources in history classes.⁶³ Despite the fact that Edwards' chapter was written over 50 years ago, his observations are still relevant, and they are briefly outlined in table 19.1 (overleaf).

I would argue that there are other common ways that sources feature in history classrooms. Perhaps most obviously, they can be a way to extend student understanding of a topic. For example, students might be reaching the end of a unit of work and be given the opportunity to find new source material that adds new knowledge and perspectives to the topic. The development of

---

61 Peter Lee, "Historical Knowledge and the National Curriculum", in Bourdillon, H. (ed.) *Teaching History*, Routledge, 1994, p. 45.
62 Stéphane Lévesque, *Thinking Historically: Educating Students for the 21st Century*, University of Toronto Press, 2008, p. 130.
63 A. D. Edwards, "Source Material in the Classroom" in Burston, W. H., and Green, C. W. (eds.) *Handbook for History Teachers* (2nd Ed.), Methuen Education Ltd, 1972, pp. 207-14.

world-class databases such as the National Library of Australia's *Trove* website (https://trove.nla.gov.au/), which has millions of newspaper articles digitised and electronically searchable, has only opened these opportunities up further.

TABLE 19.1: Common uses of sources in history classes (A. D. Edwards)

Stimulus	Often, history teachers use and explore sources with students that provide vivid insights into the material that they are exploring. These might come in the form of photography, rich descriptions and eye-witness perspectives to a major event or individual. This can often form excellent lesson starters such as See, Think, Wonder activities to draw students into the learning.
Interrogation	Teachers might also want students to closely analyse a particular source by exploring issues such as its origins, context and perspective. They would often also go further and attempt to find some useful evidence within the source that might open up new insights into the topic they are exploring.
Constructing	One of the most "realistic" activities students can be required to complete in relation to historical sources is the process of constructing a description, narrative or argument about the past informed by specific evidence gathered from sources. This process of "putting history back together" can often be far more interesting than processes of deconstructing and critiquing sources.
Contest	Encountering sources may also introduce contest to history, particularly if sources conflict in their description or interpretation of an event. Though it can be difficult to resolve these contested interpretations, this can also add new intrigue to a topic and add academic depth to students' work.

Each of these examples is far more intentional and intelligent than simply requiring students to "do another source analysis". They also have a much greater chance of sustaining student interest, helping them develop richer substantive and disciplinary knowledge, and ensuring that working with sources does not become a dreary exercise in filling out another template (though templates and scaffolds may also have their place in these processes).

Insights from research

Research into history teaching has been robust for decades. Though far from conclusive, many investigations have produced useful insights into how working with sources in secondary school history classes might be improved.

Perhaps most foundational to modern thinking about how to work with sources in the context of secondary history has been the research of Professor Sam Wineburg. His articles throughout the 1990s and then his book *Historical Thinking and Other Unnatural Acts* (2001) have had a profound influence on the way many history educators in different parts of the world frame their work.

Some of the key insights of the education research into teaching history with source material were summarised by Abby Reisman and Sarah McGrew in an excellent chapter "Reading in History Education: Text, Sources and Evidence" in *The Wiley International Handbook of History Teaching and Learning* (2018).[64] There are briefly outlined in Table 19.2, but the entire chapter is well worth reading.

TABLE 19.2: Some insights from academic research into the use of sources in secondary history education (discussed in Reisman and McGrew)

Study	Summary of key insights
Wineburg (1991 and 1994)	Highlights the significant differences between the way "experts" (historians) and "novices" (students) approach and then read primary documents. Even historians with less background knowledge in an area of history can still begin to formulate reasonable conclusions about sources given their reading and analytical strategies. This differs from students who demonstrate much simpler reading strategies.
De La Paz (2005)	Modelling, guided practice and "fading" improve key aspects of students' reasoning and writing with sources (though not necessarily their reading practices).
Notes, Dole and Hacker (2007)	Students exposed to multiple documents, instead of isolated or single texts, improve their work with sources and their knowledge of the topic.
Van Boxtel and Van Drie (2012)	Deeper historical knowledge allows students to read documents and sources with greater complexity. "Reading" or "source criticism" strategies are more useful for students when they are taught in conjunction with deep content knowledge.

---

64 Abby Reisman and Sarah McGrew, "Reading in History Education: Text, Sources and Evidence", in Metzger, S., and Harris, L. (eds.) *The Wiley International Handbook of History Teaching and Learning*, John Wiley and Sons, 2018, pp. 529-50.

Study	Summary of key insights
Reisman (2012)	This study demonstrates that work with sources improves students' knowledge and analytical work when the structure of the teaching revolves around: (a) Building background knowledge, (b) Working with modified primary sources, and, (c) Whole-class discussion.

Other qualitative research into the use of sources in secondary history has also revealed a range of helpful insights. Most notably, in my view, Jamie Byrom has stressed the importance of avoiding the trap of endless "source analysis" and deconstruction in which students critically engage with sources over and over again with little chance to create narratives and arguments with this material.[65] Too much analysis of sources without opportunities to build history might lead to cynicism, he – I think correctly – suggests.

Broad-level strategies

When considering whether to use a source (or some sources), it is useful to ask what you are trying to achieve. Is the source more for stimulus, interrogation, construction, contest or extension (see Table 19.1)? That is likely to help guide the kinds of activities you then develop.

Depending on your curriculum requirements, it may also be worth considering the topics in which sources will play a more and less prominent role. Though I generally use sources in every topic I teach, I am not convinced that every topic needs the same depth and complexity of engagement with this material. Instead, I think it can be more helpful to strategically select topics, or components of specific topics, that might feature sources more prominently.

To go a step further, we might return to the ideas set out in Table 19.1 and consider the frequency with which we expect to use these common strategies in our teaching. Some considerations for this are set out in Table 19.3.

TABLE 19.3: Frequency of the different uses of sources in secondary history

Stimulus	Most topics will give space to use sources as examples and illustrations of the content in focus. They can be excellent ways of bringing the subject to life through observation and discussion.

---

[65] Jamie Byrom, "Working with Sources: Scepticism or Cynicism? Putting the Story Back Together Again", *Teaching History*, No. 91, 1998, pp. 32-33.

Interrogation	This may be best contained in a specific topic in a stage or year. If, for example, a class studies three topics in a year, select one that offers the most logical opportunity to complete sustained interrogation of sources as one of its major themes and then complete other interrogative activities more selectively in other topics.
Constructing	Using sources as a means to the end of constructing descriptions, explanations and arguments can be done with higher frequency. It may not require formulaic processes of filling out source analysis templates, which can easily become tedious and counterproductive.
Contest	This might be used at the teacher's discretion, and there is no requirement that it be a high-frequency part of secondary history, especially in the early years. Teaching students to handle significant source discrepancies can be extremely difficult, and it requires careful planning. It can, it should be noted, also be extremely interesting for students when structured well.

Selecting material to use

In Chapter 16, we explored the idea that lesson sequences might, in varied ways, centre on content, complexity and communication. Sources can play an important role in each of these aspects of a sequence of lessons.

A source could easily be used as stimulus to launch an exploration of new content, and then a small collection of sources might be used to add complexity as the students move through the lessons. They might then be required to explicitly draw on sources they have explored when they communicate substantially about what they have learned.

As teachers, we must, however, be careful that we do not overwhelm students with source after source after source. Though we might be excited about the many sources we have found that are all relevant and interesting, it may be counter-productive to bombard the students with too many different sources – they may find it hard to develop a deep appreciation of any and may not be able to see how each fits into the larger theme(s) of the topic.

It can sometimes be more useful to select a few excellent sources and ensure that they do heavier lifting in the students' learning. When planning a unit of work, it can be useful to consider what kinds of sources would be most useful for exploring this particular topic. For example, letters and diaries might provide excellent source material when studying the conditions of battle in the First World War. When teaching about civil rights in the USA, speeches from key leaders and activists such as Martin Luther King Jr could be distinctive.

The point is to avoid a situation in which, at some random point in the topic, you select any old source to throw at the students to tick off the curriculum requirement to "do sources".

Lastly, instead of selecting a wide range of individual sources that might be explored in isolation, it can be beneficial to curate small collections for students to use as they explore key aspects of a topic. For example, when exploring the nature of battle on the Somme in 1916 during the First World War, we might get the students to explore a table of statistics showing casualty figures, one image, a contemporary report of a battle, and an individual soldier's recollection of participating in the fighting. With four sources working together, students might begin to deepen their knowledge of the issue in focus and develop a greater appreciation of the role of different source material in the historical enquiry process.

Organic over formulaic engagement with source material

We are often keen to get students working critically with source material. We know that this is a valuable exercise and it can also be interesting. There is, however, a danger that "source analysis", as it is often called, can lose a meaningful place within the process of studying history. So, how do we ensure that our work with sources does not accidentally morph into a mechanical or dreary process where students do little more than fill out templates? How do we ensure that student engagement with sources is organic and authentic rather than formulaic?

The first and perhaps most important point to stress is that students' work with sources should generally be conducted within a cohesive sequence of lessons and be guided by a clear goal that brings together relevant substantive, disciplinary and practical knowledge.[66] Professional historians certainly work with sources regularly, but they do this in the context of specific research projects that have, at their core, coherent guiding questions. Their work with sources is then framed by this project, and this helps determine their judgment of the material they grapple with.

Though we are not necessarily training mini historians in secondary schools, it would be wise to follow the lead of historians in this regard by ensuring that students have a purpose to guide their exploration of sources. This may be

---

[66] See Stéphane Lévesque, *Thinking Historically: Educating Students for the 21st Century*, University of Toronto Press, 2008, specifically Chapter 6: "How Do We Make Sense of the Raw Materials of the Past? - Evidence", pp. 112–39.

the inquiry question framing a topic or sequence of lessons (see Chapter 14) or a specifically designed question focusing student attention on key issues relating to source material.

To take one example, if we are studying the reign of Asoka the Great, who ruled the Mauryan Empire from 268 to 232 BCE, we might be asking the students to engage with the question: "What kind of ruler was Asoka the Great?"

We might then begin using the famous Edicts that Asoka created as primary source material of his reign. With the above question as our guide, we can ask: "How valuable are the Edicts to our understanding of the nature of Asoka's rule?" In this case, the purpose of exploring the Edicts is clear, and the students have a specific lens through which to analyse and work with the Edicts. They can begin to judge their value and limitations and other features of the artefacts.

If we simply asked the students what the value of the Edicts was without any overarching question or project in mind, many might become quickly lost and find it difficult to provide any insightful analysis of the material.

In short, students, like historians, should generally have a problem to solve or a question to explore if they are to work analytically and intelligently with source material.

Scaffolds

One of the key challenges of working critically with sources in secondary settings is that we are not necessarily working with students who have any particular expertise in the field of history. Many have not chosen to be in the class and may not have agreed to do the subject had they had the option.

So, we certainly need to look for ways to support those students who do not develop a deep understanding of the skills of source analysis quickly. They are likely to need lots of modelling from the teacher and scaffolds that they may refer to as they develop their confidence. Based on the work of Sam Wineburg and others, for example, it has become popular to ask students to use the concepts outlined in Diagram 19.1 (overleaf) when they engage with sources.

DIAGRAM 19.1: Some guiding themes to consider when working with historical sources

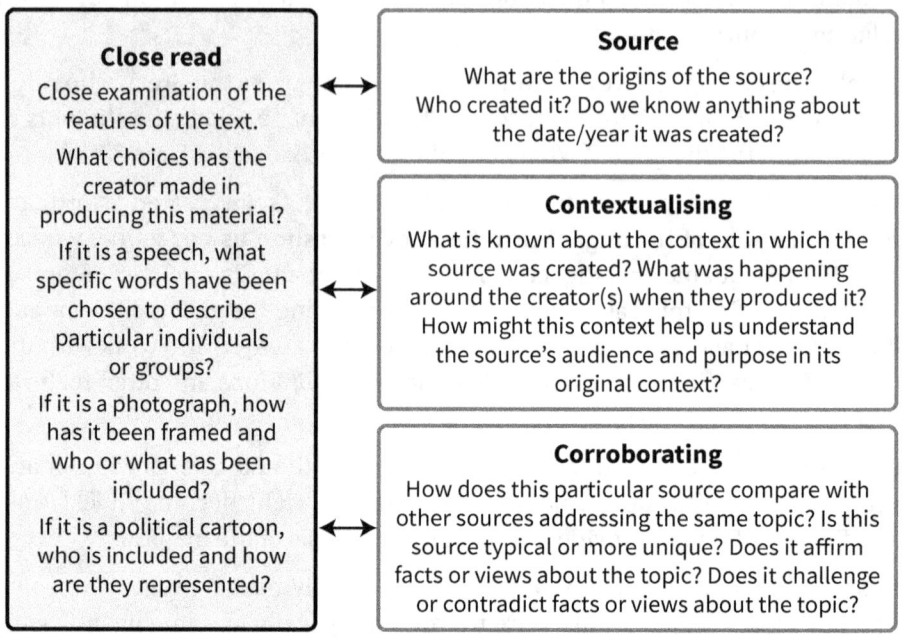

Putting it all together

Crucially, students need to be provided many opportunities to "build something worth building" when it comes to historical sources.[67] As already noted, if they perceive history to be mainly about deconstructing source material as an end in itself, they are likely to become disillusioned and unsatisfied in the process. It robs them of one of the most enjoyable aspects of history: putting it all together to say something meaningful and contest ideas.

To avoid, this, it is important to ensure that students are regularly able to respond to questions with their own narratives, descriptions and arguments that draw together their knowledge and the sources they have been working with. This can be as simple as short written pieces or brief verbal descriptions based on source material. It might be much more extended and creative work, too, including longer written or multimodal responses.

Constructing history must be done on the basis of careful work with sources and evidence. This certainly requires technical disciplinary knowledge of how to work with common sources in history. If our teaching becomes skewed

---

[67] Anna Aiken, "An Accessible, Structured Approach for Building the Intuitive Habit of Evidential Thinking Before the Examination Years", *Teaching History*, No. 168, 2017, p. 49.

towards the analytical and away from constructing the past, however, we may run the risk of accidentally turning history into a dead end for many students.

Chapter summary

- Historical sources are a crucial part of secondary history.
- Working with sources requires clarity of purpose and should generally be done within the context of coherent questions and problems that the students explore.
- Critically examining source material is important but can become mechanical if it is detached from the broader processes of developing narratives and arguments about the past.
- Scaffolds can be useful tools, but they must be used carefully to ensure that they assist, rather than hinder, students' thinking about sources and evidence.

End of chapter questions

Questions for reflection and discussion	Questions to ask experienced teachers
1. What do you like most about working with historical sources? What do you like least?	1. What are some of the most difficult aspects of teaching students to work with historical sources?
2. What are the dangers in an excessive focus on "source analysis" in secondary history?	2. How do you choose sources to work with in your classes?
3. What strategies might help avoid an overemphasis on source deconstruction?	

Further reading

Resource	Why bother reading it?
Sam Wineburg, "Historical Problem Solving: A Study of the Cognitive Processes Used in the Evaluation of Documentary and Pictorial Evidence", *Journal of Educational Psychology*, Vol. 83, No. 1, 1991, pp. 73–87	Wineburg's 1991 article is considered one of the seminal works contributing to our understanding of how sources may best be worked with in secondary school settings. It is worth reading alongside some of his others works, including the book *Historical Thinking and Other Unnatural Acts* (2001).

Resource	Why bother reading it?
Jamie Byrom, "Scepticism or Cynicism? Putting the Story Back Together Again", *Teaching History*, No. 91, May 1998, pp. 32–33	This brief article outlines some excellent approaches to ensuring that source work is productive rather than endlessly "critical".
Rosalyn Ashby, "Understanding Historical Evidence" in Ian Davies (ed.) *Debates in History Teaching (2nd Ed.)*, Routledge, pp. 144–54	Ashby sets out some helpful foundational thinking on the role of sources in secondary history. This would be particularly useful to read alongside Stéphane Lévesque's chapter discussed below.
John Whitehouse, "The Role of Questions and Sources in Promoting Historical Thinking", in Allender, T., Clark, A., and Parkes, R. (eds.) *Historical Thinking for History Teachers*, Allen & Unwin, 2019, pp. 60–71	Whitehouse outlines some ways in which questions and sources might be brought together in a productive manner to deepen students' appreciation of the process of inquiry in history.
Stéphane Lévesque, *Thinking Historically: Educating Students for the 21st Century*, University of Toronto Press, 2008 (Chapter 6: "How Do We Make Sense of the Raw Materials of the Past? – Evidence", pp. 112–39)	This chapter outlines some helpful ideas for working with historical sources in schools. It covers a range of theoretical and practical considerations and is an excellent place to start if you are seeking another overview of the place of sources in secondary history.

CHAPTER 20

Engage with historical interpretations meaningfully

Historical interpretations are a powerful and important dimension of secondary history. At a fundamental level, interpretations shape the content included in the history curriculum, but they also help to bring the subject to life for both teachers and students by providing key insights into how history is made, represented and contested.

Teachers can use historical interpretations practically to refine and expand their own subject knowledge and also to clarify what is possible to explore when teaching specific topics. Knowing what questions, debates, evidence and ideas historians have foregrounded in relevant historical sub-fields can create new ideas for topics, lesson sequences and assessment tasks.

Exploring well-placed and accessible interpretations (or versions of them) can also illuminate for students some of the ways in which aspects of the past have been critically and creatively interpreted by historians over time. Not only can this be a fascinating and enjoyable aspect of history, it can also help to sharpen students' thinking and analysis when they are required to communicate about the past. An awareness of prominent interpretations of key historical issues can help students appreciate where their own ideas come from and how their own interpretations might be similar and/or different to others.

At a more abstract level, working with historical interpretations can also provide some insights into the nature of history. In some cases, interpretations can reveal important processes and decisions that contribute to the construction of history. They can also alert students to tempting errors of analysis or representation and perhaps even point to ways in which history can be more openly abused for more sinister purposes.

All this is to say that exploring historical interpretations can help to enhance students' substantive and disciplinary knowledge.[68] Working with historical interpretations can, however, be another challenging dimension of teaching secondary history, and it requires thoughtful planning.

Appreciating historical interpretations

Research into students' perceptions of historical interpretations reveals interesting insights into the range of preconceived ideas that they might bring to history classes in secondary school. Peter Lee and Denis Schemilt point out, for example, that many students arrive at their study of history with views ranging from the defeatist ("nothing can be really known about the past") to the absolutist ("there must be only one true account of the past").[69]

In fact, a more complex and mature understanding of history would suggest that historical interpretations are possible, complex and useful for thinking about the past. Interpretations can be more complementary or contradictory, and a working knowledge of how they are created and shared offers powerful tools for confronting the past and the present.[70]

To begin to make use of historical interpretations, we first have to consider what we need to focus our attention on in secondary history settings. Arthur Chapman has helpfully argued that two major dimensions of historical interpretations are important in this context: the claims of interpretations and the factors shaping interpretations.[71] These are briefly outlined in Table 20.1.

TABLE 20.1: Two crucial dimensions of historical interpretations

Claims	It is crucial to understand the key claims offered by historical interpretations. This includes comprehending the claims, but also comparing and contrasting them to alternatives.
Factors shaping interpretations	Analysing and evaluating the way interpretations have been constructed is often more complex than comprehending and comparing their claims. It can involve exploring the role of context and authorial biography, the selection and use of evidence, the logic of arguments, and more.

---

68 Arthur Chapman, "Historical Interpretation as the Foundational Concept for History Education", *Revista de Historia (Concepción)*, Vol. 31, 2024, p. 3.
69 Peter Lee and Denis Schemilt, "'I Just Wish We Could Go Back in the Past and Find Out What Really Happened': Progression in Understanding about Historical Accounts", *Teaching History*, Vol. 117, 2004, p. 26.
70 Arthur Chapman, "Historical Interpretations", in Davies, I. (ed.) *Debates in History Teaching*, Routledge, 2017, pp. 100-12.
71 Arthur Chapman, "Historical Interpretations", pp. 106-8.

Making use of the differing claims of historical interpretations

One powerful way to begin introducing secondary students to historical interpretations is to provide accessible insights into varying claims made about key questions and themes. Juxtaposing interpretative claims can help them develop greater appreciation of the ways in which interpretations can be used constructively to build a rich tapestry of insights into the past.

To take one concrete example, consider various interpretations of the Tet Offensive launched by communist forces during the Vietnam War in January 1968. The series of dramatic surprise attacks on urban centres of South Vietnam failed to meet the main objectives of its architects – to overthrow the South Vietnamese government – but it is often cited as a key "turning point" of the conflict. Some historians emphasise the political fallout from the attacks in the United States, some stress the offensive's impact on the military dynamics of the conflict, and other historians underscore its consequences for international diplomacy and for the leadership in North and South Vietnam.[72]

Even a basic understanding of these different claims offered by historians can enrich students' analysis of the historical significance of the Tet Offensive. Importantly, this does not necessarily require students to develop deep knowledge about how the interpretations were produced. Nor does it necessarily require them to decide between the conclusions as though one account were the true account. In fact, many of the claims about the Tet Offensive's significance identified above are complementary in that they stress and illuminate different consequences of the Tet Offensive. Collectively, the claims that these historians make provide a broader appreciation of the Tet Offensive's overall importance to the Vietnam War because they trace different outcomes to create a richer impression of cause and consequence.

There are also many contradictory claims made about the impact and legacies of the Tet Offensive. For example, some recent historians have claimed that the offensive actually strengthened the South Vietnamese government, whereas others are not so convinced. Adjudicating between these interpretations presents another, more complex opportunity to debate and contest the past, requiring students to consider which historian may have better evidence to support their conclusions.

Many of the best questions we explore with our secondary history classes are not new, and gathering and exploring the claims historians have made

---

72 Jonathon Dallimore, "The Tet Offensive: Contesting Change and Continuity in the Vietnam War", *Teaching History*, Vol. 57, No. 1, 2023, pp. 19–22.

about these problems can provide a powerful introduction to some of the most insightful thinking of those who have gone before us. Some further considerations for using complementary conclusions in secondary history are outlined in Table 20.2.

TABLE 20.2: Other considerations for exploring the claims of historical interpretations

How many?	How many different interpretative claims you might place before a class depends on a range of factors, including the students' age and confidence, your own access to useful interpretations, and the nature of the topic or issue itself. Sometimes two conclusions can be sufficient, but this can also be limiting or run the risk of giving students the impression that there are only two ways to see a historical problem when that may be inaccurate.
When to explore the interpretations?	Alternative claims of interpretations can be introduced at any stage of a topic or sequence of lessons. It can be done towards the end once students have developed strong substantive knowledge to deepen their analysis of a key question or theme. It can also be done towards the beginning of a topic or sequence of lessons to introduce a key question or problem that the students are required to engage with.
Types of history	Different types of academic history can be useful for exploring interpretative claims. For example, historians focused mainly on political or economic issues may provide different conclusions to social or cultural historians. Historians interested in larger and smaller scales of time or geography might also offer some interesting opportunities to juxtapose interpretations.
Expanding student knowledge and experience	Exploring varied claims about a central question or issue can be an excellent opportunity to allow students greater freedom to research and expand their own understanding. In this situation, a teacher might work through one or two sample interpretations and then require the students to conduct research to find and share additional interpretations. This can allow students to consolidate their ability to conduct historical research and also add interesting variety into the classroom as the students bring new interpretations to a discussion.

I often introduce competing conclusions framed around key historical concepts such as causation or change and continuity. This can help to broaden students' appreciation of the types of arguments that historians make, the kinds of evidence they use and the kinds of analytical language they might deploy in communicating their arguments about the past. For example, when reading the claims of historians about causation, we might see them using terms such as prominent, primary, central, crucial and peripheral to highlight the judgments they make about the relative importance of different causal factors – something I would hope that students could ultimately manage in their own causal arguments.

Investigating the factors shaping interpretations

In practical terms, developing a familiarity with factors shaping historical interpretations involves a growing appreciation of the ways in which people put their histories together and then put them to use in the world. It requires students to consider how and why people construct histories, the methods they use to develop their stories and interpretations of the past, the forms in which they choose to communicate, and ethical considerations of presenting the past in different ways.

Because this can be time-consuming work, it may be appropriate for students to concentrate on fewer examples when exploring the factors shaping historical interpretations. This may mean that the breadth and variety of interpretations might be narrowed slightly so that students can spend more time on deeper analysis of the way an interpretation of the past was put together.

Analysing interpretations involves revealing and evaluating the choices individuals and groups make when representing the past. This can include establishing some contemporary context for the interpretation and then exploring the selections made in terms of topic, evidence, style and/or audience to develop a deeper appreciation of how an interpretation was produced. Questions that might help guide this kind of analysis could include:

- Who created this interpretation? Is there anything important about their life or worldview that helps makes sense of their interpretation?
- What was their aim in producing this interpretation?
- What methods were used to construct and present this interpretation?
- In what ways is this interpretation similar and different to other interpretations of the same theme or issue?
- How have others responded to this interpretation?

Again, exploring historical interpretations in this manner can open up interesting opportunities for more independent student work. Students might explore an interpretation together as a class before breaking into smaller groups to research other interpretations of the same question or issue. This can also create important opportunities for exploring a variety of interpretations and even create exciting new opportunities to pursue as students find interpretations the teacher and other students were not aware of.

It is important to remember too that interpretations can have their own powerful and interesting stories. Exploring the individuals and groups who produce history, the way they put their interpretations together, and how they use these to shape public understanding of the past can be dramatic and intriguing. Powerful stories are not the preserve of past historical personalities; they can also be found in the creation of and contest over historical interpretations.

History beyond historians

As argued in Chapter 3, an appreciation of the ways in which histories are made and used might be seen as one of the key goals of secondary history. Whether we like it or not, we live in a world so saturated by the past – films, political polemics, TikTok influencers, and street names all make use of the past – that some knowledge of how to handle these various forms of history seems as crucial as ever.

The Australian historian Greg Dening tried to capture this problem when he argued that all histories were performances of some kind.[73] He tried to embody the complexity of this notion in his scholarship and teaching by taking seriously the responsibilities of deep and thoughtful academic research while also believing that history always has some theatrical element as writers, teachers and creators necessarily select, structure and style their work for varied audiences. As he wrote in an essay for the journal *History and Theory*:

> History – the past transformed into words or paint or dance or play – is always a performance. An everyday performance as we present our selective narratives about what has happened at the kitchen table, to the courts, to the taxman, at the graveside.[74]

History is performed by actors for a film, by parents as they try to relate aspects of their family's past to their children, and by the curators of museum exhibitions who carefully arrange objects, labels and lighting to evoke particular responses. History is also performed, Dening argues, by academics who arrange highly technical displays of their thinking about the past often in large, densely written books filled with footnotes and sources.

---

73 See Greg Dening, *Performances*, University of Chicago Press, 1996, and Tom Griffith, *The Art of Time Travel: Historians and Their Craft*, Black Inc. Books, 2016, pp. 76–87.
74 Greg Dening, "Performing on the Beaches of the Mind: An Essay", *History and Theory*, Vol. 41, No. 1, 2002, p. 1.

An awareness of the various ways in which history is and can be performed can deepen students' appreciation of how history works in and beyond the discipline, but it can also empower them beyond the classroom as they confront histories in their everyday life.

The point here is not to overwhelm students by inundating them with a dizzying array of histories. Rather, it is to consider how and when we might explore historical interpretations delivered outside the confines of academic scholarship in addition to more-traditional forms of disciplinary work.

Planning to include interpretations

The previous chapter argued that it is important to plan for intentional and strategic use of sources in secondary history. The same needs to be stressed when approaching historical interpretations. As a start, it is worth considering more macro-level planning about interpretations and then more topic-specific planning.

Macro-level planning for this aspect of teaching secondary history involves stepping back from lessons and sequences to consider the place of interpretations across whole-year and stage levels. Though you may not decide to conduct a deep investigation of constructions of history in every topic, you might choose to ensure that a case study of this kind is incorporated into each year or stage of your teaching plan.

TABLE 20.3: One possible plan for introducing students to a variety of historical interpretations over the course of several years of secondary history (note that students would also engage with other interpretations in other topics, but these would form more sustained case studies)

	Interpretation focus	Brief description
Year 7	Museum exhibition	Students might explore the way a museum exhibition has interpreted the role of a key individual from the ancient world they have studied in class. If possible, they might visit the exhibition and then present in small groups to the class.
Year 8	Film study	Towards the end of a unit, students may watch a prominent film engaging with key aspects of the topic. They might then read about the creation of the film and consider critiques of its interpretation before writing a film review targeting its historical interpretation.

	Interpretation focus	Brief description
Year 9	Popular history	Students may be given opportunities to select a popular representation of history in the form of a book, game or film and be required to conduct more in-depth research into its interpretation of a key aspect of history. They might then present their analyses to the class.
Year 10	Academic history	As the students' knowledge and confidence about history grows, they might be required to complete a more sustained investigation into the way one or two academic historians differ in their interpretations of a key question or issue they have explored in class.

Topic-specific planning would then involve considering which interpretations to prioritise across each topic completed. These may not require deep studies but should at least introduce a range of conclusions that help students appreciate the complexity of views on the issues raised in each topic. To do this, it can be helpful to ask some questions that might guide your selection, such as:

- Are there historians or interpretations that have defined this particular field that are worth exploring?
- Are there any historians or interpretations that might provide useful counterpoints or additions to the material the students will explore through their textbooks or other common resources?
- Are there any historians or interpretations that might raise interesting observations or questions that could help pique student interest in the topic?

The crucial aim of planning to incorporate historical interpretations into teaching secondary history is to ensure that students get the opportunity to explore different kinds of historical interpretations over time. In that process, we would hope that their ability to work with interpretations in academic and non-academic forms might grow and, along with it, their general historical confidence and agility.

Chapter summary

- Historical interpretations are a crucial dimension of history and history education.
- Exploring historical interpretations can assist students in developing their historical knowledge and understanding and their meta-historical knowledge and understanding.
- Exploring different claims made by historical interpretations is one important dimension of secondary history that can enrich student thinking about substantive and disciplinary knowledge.
- Deeper analysis of historical interpretations involves exploring the factors shaping their construction, including the aims of interpretations, the stories behind how they were developed, the methods and sources used, the audiences for which interpretations were produced, and their reception.
- It is important to plan to incorporate historical interpretations across year levels and stages and also within specific topics.

End of chapter questions

Questions for reflection and discussion	Questions to ask experienced teachers
1. How can an understanding of historical interpretations assist teachers as they plan to teach secondary history? 2. How can studying historical interpretations help students studying secondary history? 3. What is the difference between exploring contrasting conclusions and studying differing constructions of history? 4. Use Table 20.2 as a starting point to develop a draft for including historical interpretations in a macro-level teaching plan for the curriculum you will be teaching.	1. How do you incorporate historical interpretations into your teaching? 2. Do you take students to museums or historic sites as a way of exploring historical interpretations? How do you use this?

Further reading

Resource	Why bother reading it?
Arthur Chapman, "Historical Interpretations", in Davies, I. (ed.) *Debates in History Teaching*, Routledge, 2017, pp. 100–12	Chapman's discussion of the role of historical interpretations in secondary history in *Debates in History Teaching* provides some important ideas about what interpretations we might explore and how we might do this. It balances conceptual and theoretical considerations with practical ideas for evaluating interpretations.
Christine Baron, "Understanding Historical Thinking at Historic Sites", *Journal of Educational Psychology*, Vol. 104, No. 3, 2012, pp. 833–47	Baron's research was conducted at a site in Boston (USA) and suggests some strategies for interpreting historic sites.
Debra Donnelly, "Integrating Filmic Pedagogies into the Teaching and Learning Cycle", in Allender, T., Clark, A., and Parkes, R. (eds.) *Historical Thinking for History Teachers*, Allen & Unwin, 2019, pp. 221–30	Debra Donnelly considers how and why historical films might be used in secondary history classes.
Jonathon Dallimore, "The Tet Offensive: Contesting Change and Continuity in the Vietnam War", *Teaching History*, Vol. 57, No. 1, 2023, pp. 19–22	This article provides an introduction to a range of historical interpretations of the 1968 Tet Offensive during the Vietnam War. It demonstrates how the claims of historical interpretations can be used to help students refine their own thinking and analysis about change and continuity.
Arthur Chapman, "Multiperspectivity and Monuments", HISTOLAB Tutorial: https://histolab.coe.int/activities/tutorials	This video tutorial offers some practical advice on how we might explore historical monuments as interpretations in secondary history.

CHAPTER 21

Use particular pedagogies to solve subject problems

One key aim of this book has been to place subject-specific challenges and opportunities of teaching secondary history at the forefront of our thinking. Although general pedagogical principles are extremely important to consider when teaching any subject, if these ideas begin to overshadow unique disciplines, my worry is that the aims and nature of the subject can quickly fade into the background.

Consider this scenario. A history teacher becomes keen on the idea that students of the 21st century should know some computer coding – this was all the rage in the 2010s. So, they are determined to embed some coding in history to support that goal. They come up with the idea of getting the students to code a small history quiz game on school-supplied software. The students spend three weeks learning the coding language and produce a short quiz game on their latest topic which asks five multiple-choice questions. The students code into the quiz wacky and entertaining responses from the platform when a respondent answers incorrectly – bursting balloons, large flashing text sweeping the screen spelling out the word "FAIL", and so on.

In this scenario, some likely outcomes are possible. First, some students may genuinely enjoy the activity and they may be highly active across the three weeks given to the task, perhaps more active than they have ever been in this class at other times. Second, students may be mostly well-behaved. Third, some students may have learned new ideas relating to computer coding and demonstrated some impressive ability to manipulate the platform. Fourth, they may have revised a few aspects of their learning in history by designing the five-question multiple-choice quiz game requiring them to ask clear questions and decide on correct answers. None of these are undesirable in and of themselves.

What is unclear, however, is how much history these students have learned in the three weeks of the activity. How has their substantive and disciplinary knowledge or their ability to communicate about the past grown over that not-insignificant period? Though it is difficult to be certain, one might suspect that most students have not progressed too far in these areas.

The danger then is that history seems to have become a secondary concern to coding when it should have been the other way around. Instead of technology enlivening and enriching history, the subject appears to have been overshadowed to at least some degree by computer coding.

This is certainly not to say that technology and history are always in competition, but, when used like this, they can seem to be. To avoid that, we would do well to always ask: "How might this particular pedagogical initiative or approach expand and improve the goals of this unique subject and the topic(s) we are focused on?" Not, "How could I throw this or that into the mix of my history lessons to jazz them up a bit?" And to be clear, there may be robustly justifiable grounds on which to work with history through coding, but, for me, they would have to be more thoughtful than the scenario described above.

Group work in history

Group work is not new and nor is opposition to it. Some teachers use it regularly and others almost never, if at all. Some initial teacher education courses and some schools place a heavy emphasis on it, while others do not. This can leave many early-career teachers wondering where it might fit in their pedagogical repertoire.

If group work is done solely because you believe that it is generally important for students to learn to collaborate, there is a possibility that history will suffer as a result. There is no guarantee that learning history through group work will always be better or preferable and, if the group task takes considerable time, there is always the lingering question: was it worth it?

So, it might be better to begin with a question that helps us ensure that the subject, history, remains the focus of our considerations: is there an element of this topic that group work will enhance? In many situations, we may conclude that group work will be beneficial, but we might also conclude that it would be more of a distraction and decide to use a different strategy.

Still, there are some common aspects of history in which group work can be useful because it enriches important aspects of the subject. Some of these are outlined in Table 21.1.

In each of the scenarios outlined in Table 21.1, group work is enhancing the subject, not distracting from or confusing it. They are not the only logical uses of group work in history, but they are common.

TABLE 21.1: Meaningful uses of group work in history

Sources	In some topics, a wide range of sources may be available, and it may not matter too much which ones students engage with. In this scenario, it could be useful to model intelligent investigation of the material and then get students to explore different sources in groups and discuss their findings. The variety may enhance the students' overall impressions of what they are learning, and it would be difficult or even impossible to achieve this with a narrower activity focused on one or two sources mostly controlled by the teacher.
Perspectives	When exploring different perspectives of an event, individual or issue, it could be logical to get students to explore a response from the viewpoint of a specific individual or group. This might mean that groups initially focus on just one unique perspective and begin to develop a deeper understanding of this before looking at alternatives. After some group reports and class discussion of the various viewpoints, students may then be required to broaden their understanding by examining other perspectives in more detail. There may be no need for them to develop deep knowledge of all the perspectives explored across the class, so a sampling is sufficient.
Individuals and groups	In some topics, we are required to explore the impact of a major development and event across a range of groups or individuals. For example, in exploring the Industrial Revolution, we might be required to examine its impact on workers, women and children (or a similar collection of different groups). Instead of teaching linearly through each one, we might explore one in depth with the students as a model and then allow them to select one in groups to explore and report on. There may not be a need for them to learn about each group in equal depth, so with this activity, the students may learn about one in significant depth and one or two others in less detail. At the end of the activity, students should have a detailed understanding of two groups (the one explored with the teacher and the one explored in their group) and a more general understanding of a third, which could be plenty.

Events	Similarly, in some topics, we might have the option to select an event from a list of possibilities as a case study for a larger theme. For example, we might be required to select a major battle from a war to explore in depth. Instead of choosing for the class and just doing one together, the teacher might provide a brief overview of several battles and then break the students into groups and get each to explore a different battle before reporting back to the class. This will mean that students develop a reasonable knowledge about one battle but also hear about a range of others, providing a balance between breadth of understanding and depth of knowledge provided by their case study.
Developing arguments and ideas	When trying to help students get used to building historical arguments, it is often a helpful approach to dialogue questions through discussion before asking the students to write at length. This helps consolidate their thinking before they set out to write. Although whole-class discussion could be a good mechanism for sharpening students' argumentative ideas, small groups could also be a helpful context to begin exploring what they think and how it might be similar or different to their peers. Not only does this provide the teacher with some excellent opportunities to see how the students' thinking is developing, it can also provide students with new ideas that they can add to their own.

Technology in history

Technology has an awkward relationship with education.[75] On the one hand, technological tools can genuinely make learning easier and more engaging. Cloud-based software platforms have made organising and sharing material among teachers far more efficient and I am genuinely excited by what augmented and virtual reality can do to enliven history classes if they are used critically and intelligently.

At the same time, edtech (educational technology) can be gimmicky and open students and the educational system up to privacy issues and exploitation in the interests of corporate profits. It does not take a jaded cynic to wonder why major technology companies are so interested in the education "market". Millions of teachers and students engage with devices, platforms and software on a daily basis all around the world. The potential for profits is enormous.

Approaching these issues soberly has become increasingly difficult in the face of mass marketing by edtech businesses. Though hardened cynicism

---

75 See, for example, Audrey Watters, *Teaching Machines: The History of Personalized Learning*, MIT Press, 2023, and Neil Selwyn, "Minding Our Language: Why Education and Technology is Full of Bullshit… and What Might Be Done About It", *Learning, Media and Technology*, Vol. 41, No. 3, 2016, pp. 437–43.

can be unhealthy, we should not be naïve to the fact that economics often plays a major role in the marketing of innovation in education.[76] It works in the companies' favour if schools and teachers feel anxious that they would be doing a disservice to students or would be "falling behind" if they did not provide ever more opportunities for students to engage with technology. Rushing into the latest wave of technological advances has, however, produced a range of dead-end experiences in education with mixed results. Because of all this, it would seem sensible, as far as possible, to approach these issues with both an open mind and a healthy sense of scepticism.

For history teachers, a more specific concern, as my story about coding earlier in the chapter tried to demonstrate, is that it is easy for history to be lost or pushed into the background if more generic edtech goals become too pronounced. The solution is certainly not to avoid technology, since it brings with it many potential benefits and since history now lives in exciting ways on many digital platforms, but to ensure that we are using it to enhance and promote the teaching and learning of history by placing the subject first.

Some simple but effective uses of edtech that can support the learning of history are outlined in Table 21.2 (overleaf).

Importantly for history teachers, specific technologies can also be a rich and robust focus for analysis with students. Films, for example, have long been an object of study in history classes. But, increasingly, video games and other platforms have, for better or worse, also emerged as an important source of students' ideas about the past.[77] Some teachers have worked closely with incorporating technologies such as video games into secondary education.[78] Here the idea is not simply to use video games to engage students about the past, although that can be possible too, it is also to use material that many students engage with regularly to deepen their historical thinking about the past through this media.

Technology can also assist teachers as they help students deepen their historical understanding and analysis. Janet van Drie and Carla van Boxtel have, for example, developed interesting strategies for using online tools for developing students' ability to form arguments in the context of writing essays.[79] Others have explored the opportunities and pitfalls in using social media platforms to enrich students' understanding of representation of

---

76 For a general discussion of the role of marketing and competition in Australian education, for example, see Craig Campbell and Helen Proctor, *A History of Australian Schooling*, Allen & Unwin, 2014, pp. 211-47.
77 A. Martin Wainwright, *Virtual History: How Video Games Portray the Past*, Routledge, 2019.
78 See, for example, Jeremiah McCall's website "Gaming the Past" and his accompanying book: https://gamingthepast.net/
79 Janet van Drie and Carla van Boxtel, "Chatting About the Sixties: Historical Reasoning in Essay-writing" *Teaching History*, Vol. 140, 2010, pp. 38-46.

colonial history.[80] This is to say nothing of the dizzying array of commentary now available about generative artificial intelligence and education.

These examples only begin to hint at the creative and powerful possibilities for using technology to enliven secondary history without compromising the deeper aims of the subject.

TABLE 21.2: Meaningful uses of technology in history

Research	Perhaps most obviously, easily accessible scholarly databases can be a rich opportunity for students to complete research-based assessment tasks. Though students need to be shown how to use these effectively, they can be a great asset for history teachers. See below for a longer discussion of research.
Drafting	The ready access to artificial intelligence platforms that have proliferated in recent times has added many new opportunities for history teachers, along with a range of threats to their work. Some artificial intelligence platforms can be used to help students draft clear research questions and even begin the process of ideation and refining expression. Here, clear rules around plagiarism need to be set out, but used thoughtfully, these platforms can provide additional tools that help achieve the aims of the subject.
Assessments	Some excellent major assessments include at least one dimension of technology. For example, instead of delivering a speech in person (useful in its own right), students might be required to make a multimedia presentation including student narration and analysis along with images and footage combined into a short film.
Collaboration	In small-group tasks, cloud-based software can be easily leveraged for students to collaborate. For example, students might work on an online document to annotate source material or collate their ideas as a group. In other scenarios they might use a template to generate insights from research to share with the class.

Research in history

Research is a cherished aspect of history. In fact, it might be considered to be one of the pillars of the academic discipline itself. Just as there are dangers with other more generic pedagogical ideas such as group work and technology, however, research in history also needs to be used intentionally and intelligently to ensure that the subject is not overshadowed.

---

80 Everardo Perez-Manjarrez, "'It Isn't About Who Was Worse': Colonialism and Historical Debate on Social Media", in Carretero, M., Cantabrana, M., and Parellada, C. (eds.) *History Education in the Digital Age*, Springer, 2022, pp. 125–41.

Thinking back over my early career, I remember getting students to research information about a topic on computers because I thought this was "doing history". And yet, I found that if the students did not already have strong content knowledge or research confidence, they often ended up finding a mix of useful, incorrect and strange information – a reasonable learning exercise in itself. In some cases, I also realised that it would have been better to just use a textbook to work through this content with the students, since the process and the results of the research were not particularly rich or useful.

It is also wise to consider what we really mean by research. Is it gathering information from a Wikipedia page? Is it using a more formalised library database to find extended and technical texts? Is it using an online trove of sources to find material to deepen student knowledge? For me, the latter two examples generally fit my instincts more closely, and I rarely, if ever, use the former except to fill in some gaps that may have appeared in the resources the class has been using.

Some common ways that student research might be used in secondary history are outlined in Table 21.3.

TABLE 21.3: Meaningful uses of research in history

Technical research	With older students, you might get them to collect several books and articles from a library for a major research-based assessment task. This could involve work with a librarian exploring how to use databases or other indexes.
Sources	I often provide students with the sources that I want them to use, but I will sometimes also use a research activity so that students have some experience of gathering them too. These activities can include fairly structured tasks in which I might get the students to explore a specific collection or database rather than complete a general search. For example, in Australia we have Trove, run by the National Library, which holds thousands of digitised articles and other items to explore. I have done some excellent local history research activities using Trove, and it can be a brilliant opportunity to experience the joy of finding surprising material and the challenge of working with material that stretches, changes or expands students' understanding. I would usually do this after the students have already begun to develop deep knowledge about the issue we are exploring. It can also be fascinating to remove the barriers on student research and see what they find in a more open process. Students can often find unpredictable and very unique material that broadens the themes and issues explored by the class. This can be exciting and is a good reminder that history is not always predictable.

Filling in gaps	On occasion, I might get my class to do a mini-research session to fill in some important gaps in their understanding. For example, we might be working through a topic, and I might realise that the materials I have prepared are missing some important substantive knowledge. So I might decide to conduct a quick research activity to get the students to fill in this knowledge and move deeper into the topic.
Contemporary perspectives	I have also used more spontaneous research activities when a contemporary event might be connected to what students are learning. For example, I recall teaching when Fidel Castro died. I had a class use the news function on Google to look up examples of the headlines and see if they could quickly detect varying perspectives and then use the examples that they found to begin discussing why these reactions might be present. This became the basis for a larger activity on assessing Castro's historical significance. These kinds of activities may not necessarily be used regularly, but it is worth always remaining open to possibilities.

Chapter summary

- Generic pedagogical tools and approaches such as group work, technology and research can be useful mechanisms to support the teaching and learning of history.
- These can also distract from the subject when not used thoughtfully, reflectively and critically.
- It is always best to ask: "How might these tools and approaches enhance and improve the teaching and learning of history?"

End of chapter questions

Questions for reflection and discussion	Questions to ask experienced teachers
1. How can generic pedagogical approaches overshadow history in secondary settings? 2. In what ways can teachers ensure that the subject, history, remains central in activities using group work, technology or research? 3. How did you experience group work, technology and research as a student in secondary school? Did you enjoy it? Were there cases in which it was used in more and less helpful ways?	1. What are some of the common ways in which you use group work, technology and research in your secondary history classes? 2. How do you ensure that students remain engaged and active during group work activities? 3. Do any of the major assessment tasks that you often use require major use of technology? How do you manage these?

Further reading

Resource	Why bother reading it?
Tom Sherrington, "Pedagogy Postcard 9: Group Work", 4 April 2014: : https://teacherhead.com/2014/04/04/pedagogy-postcard-9-group-work/	This brief post has some excellent reflections on and suggestions for using group work in schools. Although it is not entirely dedicated to history teaching, there are strong and thoughtful principles discussed and some history-specific examples too.
Terry Haydn, "Hard Choices: What Does It Mean 'To Be Good at ICT' as a History Educator? A View From England", in Carretero, M., Cantabrana, M., and Parellada, C. (eds.) *History Education in the Digital Age*, Springer, 2022, pp. 29–42	Haydn outlines some of the divergent views about technology and history education. He shows that many teachers are optimistic about aspects of technology for history, but also that real concerns exist about "digital literacy", since students can access ideas about history from an ever-increasing number of sources.
James Goulding, "Using Websites to Develop Historical Thinking" in Allender, T., Clark, A., and Parkes, R. (eds.) *Historical Thinking for History Teachers*, Allen & Unwin, 2019, pp. 231–44	James Goulding's research on the use of websites in history education provides some important ideas for exploring online material in a critical and constructive manner.

Resource	Why bother reading it?
Neil Selwyn, "Minding Our Language: Why Education and Technology is Full of Bullshit… and What Might Be Done About It", *Learning, Media and Technology*, Vol. 41, No. 3, 2016, pp. 437–43	This article discusses the way educational technology can be full of hype and argues that we need to be critical consumers of the language, the software and the gadgets.
HTANSW, *Teaching History* (journal), Vol. 57, No. 3, 2022: "Artificial Intelligence"	This volume of the New South Wales *Teaching History* journal is entirely dedicated to artificial intelligence in history teaching. There are many articles and teaching ideas that might be adapted for different educational settings.
Jeremiah McCall, *Gaming the Past: Using Video Games to Teach Secondary History (2nd ed.)*, Routledge, 2022	This book includes a wide range of ideas regarding the use of videos games in history. There is also an accompanying website: https://gamingthepast.net/

CHAPTER 22

Consider weight, energy and mode in your lessons

In my early years of teaching secondary history, I regularly taught a unit of work on the Cambodian Revolution (1975-79). I was enthusiastic about this topic since I had travelled extensively throughout the region, read many books on the topic, and saw interesting and important opportunities to expand the students' understanding of 20th century revolutions through a non-European case study.

In my earnestness to get deep into the content, I remember warning a class as we began that the topic would be difficult because it dealt with significant tragedy and trauma, before launching into the content. Within a few lessons, some dedicated students came to me to explain that they were finding the material extremely difficult to process because it was so deeply confronting. They pointed out that the material was not only emotional, but also dense and complex because there were many unfamiliar groups, individuals and ideas to contend with. Their comments were, fortunately, made in a constructive spirit, as they were interested in the issues we were beginning to explore and they liked history.

When I reflect on this now, I realise that there were several errors in the way I had approached this topic with the class. I did not sufficiently prepare the students for the challenging content, for example, but I had also rushed into difficult material and kept the pace up without giving the students opportunities to slow down, discuss and safely process what they were exploring. In other words, I was so keen to develop their substantive knowledge of the Cambodian Revolution (partly because an external exam loomed at the end) that I was overwhelming the students, and it risked derailing an important topic. Thankfully, the students who had approached me with their concern alerted me to this with just enough time to adjust.

When you are a teacher interested in the subject matter and you have studied the material you teach for many years, it is easy to forget what it is like to confront some topics for the first time. It can be extremely challenging in ways that you might have forgotten. Though we cannot give the students time off from their studies in our classes, we can intelligently reflect on our practices and try to avoid burning the students out unnecessarily.

One approach to this in secondary history is to reflect on three dimensions of your lessons to try to avoid the subject becoming an unmanageable burden. These are weight, energy and mode.

Paying attention to weight

In this context, the term weight refers to the difficulty of the material that you require the students to engage with. First, this means the intellectual complexity, which may include the length and density of texts you require the students to work with, the amount of new information, and the degree of conceptual abstraction. Second, it means the emotional difficulty, which could include the nature of the content and the perspectives from which students explore a topic. At times we can teach material that is both intellectually and emotionally demanding. Sometimes the intellectual dimensions or the emotional dimensions to what we teach are more demanding.

DIAGRAM 22.1: Intellectual and emotional weight in history lessons

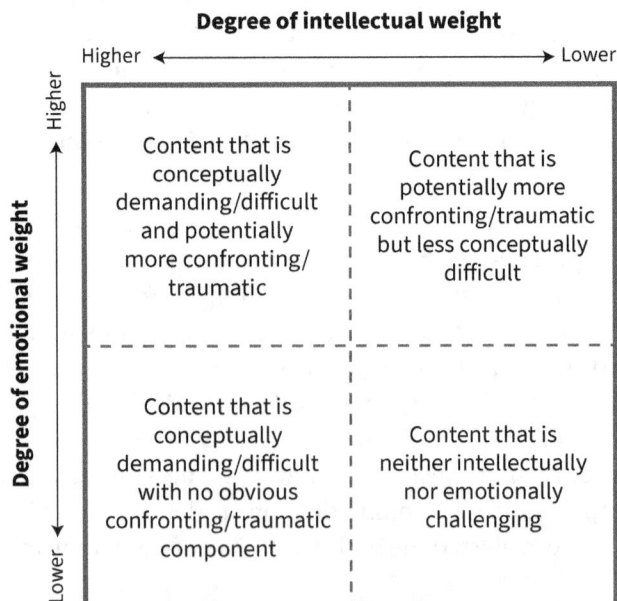

Material that has a higher degree of intellectual and/or emotional weight is more likely to tax students' working memory, so it is important to remain conscious of these dimensions of the material that we are exploring in secondary history. The point is not to eliminate all difficulties, since appropriate challenge is an important dimension of learning.[81] Instead, the point is to remain conscious of the demands we are placing on students as we work with them.

Imagine that you are teaching a Year 10 topic on post-war society exploring the way British and American influences were disseminated globally through mass popular music and film, ushering in enormous changes in many parts of the world. You get the students to read a short reflection by a member of your community on what it was like to see the Beatles for the first time. Their perspective is light-hearted and humorous, but it also raises important and useful discussion points. This is a worthwhile activity, but it is likely to be both intellectually and emotionally light in that it is probably not particularly challenging or confronting for most students. There is nothing wrong with that, since not all the content we cover should be dense and difficult.

Now, imagine that you are teaching a topic on the extremely violent Cambodian Revolution as I mentioned at the beginning of the chapter. Imagine that the students have developed a broad understanding of the main narrative, the key individuals and groups, and are beginning to explore more-complex issues through the close study of primary sources in the form of eye-witness testimony. You then require them to read longer descriptions of life under the Khmer Rouge regime from survivors that outline the impact of malnutrition, extreme violence and mass social dislocation. The language is difficult because it contains many new words with specific meanings, and the accounts are shocking because they mention the torture of innocent victims and state-sponsored murder on an unfathomable scale. In contrast to the previous example where students explore pop culture and the Beatles, this content on the Cambodian Revolution might be considered heavy, as it is both challenging to make sense of and confronting.

These examples may seem extreme, but they are not uncommon in history. Engaging with this subject means exploring topics, themes and events that can move quickly from the entertaining to the fascinating to the complex to the confronting. There is often no way around that, because that is a large part of the story of humanity.

Problems can easily arise, however, if the weight of lessons is too light or too heavy for an extended period. This was part of my mistake in the scenario

---

81 See, for example, Jade Pearce and Isaac Moore, *Desirable Difficulties in Action*, John Catt, 2024.

I described at the beginning of the chapter: too many consecutive lessons were too heavy, and I was beginning to lose students who were otherwise motivated to study history. I should have found a way to reduce the weight of some of the lessons so that they could catch their breath and continue safely and securely.

Equally, if too many lessons are intellectually light, we run the risk of losing momentum with a class. They might be enjoying the material, but they may not be developing deep or complex knowledge, and this could easily leave them behind in other ways. Higher-achieving students in this context might also quickly become bored and unmotivated.

To avoid these problematic scenarios, it is important to monitor the weight of your lessons and consider how this may be shaping the dynamics of your class(es). If you are exploring some dense medieval source material which is difficult but rewarding for the students to read, for example, this might be followed with something less intense such as a documentary or video to give the students some breathing space before you return to more-complex material. Overall, they are still making progress and your expectations remain high, but the weight varies to avoid crushing them.

It can also be worth planning ahead to try to avoid problems created by too much or too little weight in your lessons. For example, when I begin a new topic, I generally like to provide an overview of the narrative or framework in the first few lessons. In many cases, part of this would include a video or documentary that introduces and succinctly outlines key developments and themes integral to the topic. I usually require the students to respond to guided questions or take structured notes as they view these materials. It is a simple activity to organise, and useful, but it is usually not particularly dense or heavy. So, I often follow this with a more substantial reading, from a textbook or article, for example, that is more demanding. Together, the activities are hopefully productive and challenging overall, but not unnecessarily burdensome.

TABLE 22.1: Possible weight of common activities in history lessons

	Heavier	Lighter
Overview material	Longer and more substantial textbook reading with a range of new themes, terms, groups and individuals.	An overview documentary presenting a narrative of the period the class is about to investigate.

	Heavier	Lighter
Sources	Longer primary sources written in complex language and using new expressions.	Visual material or objects that students can examine to support reading or teacher exposition.
Traumatic material	Personal testimony with detailed descriptions of confronting issues. Documentaries (used with due consideration) covering confronting material with imagery or footage.	Though it may not be possible to avoid this content being heavy, depersonalising the perspective by looking at some overview text might relieve some of the weight and intensity that can come from exploring detailed eye-witness accounts.

Paying attention to energy

Paying attention to energy refers to reflecting on who is driving cognitive activity within lessons. If the teacher and one or two students in a class of 25 are most active, there is every chance that many students are simply not paying attention and are not learning much.

There is no categorical problem with a teacher standing in front of the class and explaining an important concept or modelling a procedure at length, but if this is the entire 80-minute lesson and it is repeated every lesson for two weeks, significant problems are likely to arise. One danger is that too much cognitive energy is likely to be located solely with the teacher in this scenario.

A much more effective approach would be to ensure that the energy in the lessons is more evenly distributed between the teacher and students, who should all be cognitively active throughout the lesson in different ways and in varying intensities.

The teacher

The teacher might drive the cognitive energy in a part of a lesson if they use a whiteboard and their voice to explain an important concept or model a procedure that the students will then have to use. The ideas emanate mainly from the teacher while the students (ideally) listen attentively. The students should be cognitively active as they listen, but the teacher is driving this through their explanation, modelling and questioning.

Individual students

In another part of a lesson, individual students may be working quietly on a task. Here, the teacher is still cognitively active by circulating the room, checking student progress, asking questions, and offering support where required. The students are, however, now more responsible for the cognitive activity as they engage with the material more independently and respond to whatever the task requires.

Small groups

In yet another part of a lesson, students might engage with each other through a think-pair-share activity or a larger group task. Here they are not individually engaged in a task (such as quietly reading a primary source and responding to some guided questions) but working together. Again, the teacher may be cognitively active by circulating and offering support or asking questions that prod group discussions in new directions, but this is probably less demanding than setting out a sustained explanation or demonstration of a procedure.

Whole class

Energy might be driven in a more shared sense in an activity such as a whole-class discussion. Here the teacher may be asking key questions to hear ideas, but students may also be asking questions, challenging suggestions, and elaborating on their responses to the ideas of others. When this scenario works well, it may be difficult to ultimately decipher who is driving the cognitive energy the most, as it is more evenly shared between teacher and students.

The point about these ideas is not that any of them are right or wrong, but that if over-used, any one of them could become counterproductive. In addition, an overemphasis on one may also exhaust the teacher or the students rapidly.

Though the ideal is not to strictly balance all of these in every lesson, again, it can be helpful to pay attention to who is driving the cognitive energy across your lessons and adjust this if it leans too heavily on the teacher or the students for too long.

Paying attention to mode

Mode could easily be replaced here by a term such as medium. By that, I am essentially referring to the type of resource(s) that the students are required to engage most with in a lesson. One simple example is a lesson in which students complete some substantial reading from a narrative article about the topic they are exploring as the main activity in a lesson. Here the mode would be primarily centred on written narrative text.

Given that history is dynamic, it thrives on multi-modal expression. This is not variety for variety's sake, but an authentic dimension of the discipline. History is textual, it is tactile, it is visual, it can be aural, and it can be much more besides. I would argue that sustained reading is crucial to learning history, but it would be unnecessarily limiting if that were the only mode in which students ever engaged with the past, especially given that material culture and images are so important to our understanding of many periods in history. Some useful modes for exploring history are briefly outlined in Table 22.2.

TABLE 22.2: Useful modes for exploring history

Secondary texts	Most obviously these include textbooks, articles, websites and book extracts. These are commonly used and for good reason. They can deliver rich narratives, descriptions, detail and arguments that help the students deepen their understanding of the topic.
Primary texts	Letters, diaries, newspaper articles and many other primary source texts are popular in history classes. These can be excellent for exploring contemporary perspectives, enriching students' understanding of detail and more.
Visual	Depending on the topic, this might include maps, diagrams, propaganda posters, photographs, paintings and other art, and more. Entire lessons can be built around a small selection of visual material if done so intelligently.
Audio-visual	Videos and documentaries are a wonderful resource for history teachers. The variety, quality and availability of these are probably now better than ever before. Well-made documentaries, for example, can provide varied insights into a topic through archival footage, scenery from a region in focus that may be unfamiliar to students, interviews with historians or eyewitnesses, re-enactments, and more.
Material culture	Objects can be powerful modes through which to explore the past. These could be real objects or replicas but, used thoughtfully, they can help clarify students' understanding and stimulate their imagination in ways that might otherwise be difficult.
Sites and monuments	Visiting sites can also be a powerful mode of exploring the past. For example, if students are studying the World Wars, they might visit a local monument or memorial and begin to explore questions of commemoration and memory.

There is a danger here, already hinted at above: that switching between modes becomes random or that it is done purely to keep students entertained.

This would not support genuine teaching and learning of history and it is not what I am suggesting.

Another misunderstanding here might be that I am suggesting that different modes or mediums should be used in history lessons because they might suit students' preferred "learning styles", when that is as far from my thinking as I could imagine. Rather, I have suggested that we might think here in a disciplinary sense by considering how different modes can help capture the dynamism and complexity of the past itself.

The question really is: what mode or combination of modes will bring this aspect of the topic to life and help the students deepen their understanding of this aspect of the topic most effectively? The answer will be different depending on the topic in focus, but it will probably include a combination of modes. Posing this question means that the variety then becomes an intentional rather than a random choice. Ideally, the teacher would explain why they have selected a particular mode at a particular point in a unit of work.

If, for example, I am attempting to provide the students with an overview of a new theme or issue, I tend to rely most on secondary texts and audio-visual modes such as documentaries. When I want to explore contemporary perspectives, I tend to rely more on primary texts, music or visual modes such as art.

Examples of using visual material in secondary history

When I am teaching new topics, I often try to use some visual material early on to help the students develop their knowledge of key geographic and regional issues that will repeatedly arise throughout the topic. For example, when teaching the Vietnam War, I usually work through a regional map of Southeast Asia in the first few lessons, making sure that students are aware of the locations of key regional powers, the location of key cities that are referred to extensively in textual material, and so on. I do this not because I believe that some students learn better visually, but because the map helps to make sense of key aspects of topic and a visual representation of the space is much easier and quicker to work with than a solely textual or verbal description of the region.

Often when I am teaching modern conflicts, I also make use of a lot of photographs – not necessarily violent ones, I hasten to add. Again, this is not because I think it suits some students' learning preferences, but because many students simply find it hard to imagine certain dimensions of modern conflicts because, thankfully, most have not experienced them. When we talk about the variety of the trench systems of the First World War, for example, I could get the students to read descriptions and then I could show a range of photographs and quickly explain the differences. Doing this is then likely to help the students make much quicker sense of diary entries or letters that we might use in later lessons to explore the nature of trench warfare and other themes.

In both examples, I would argue that using visual material supports important and natural dimensions of the discipline and makes working with other material such as textual sources easier. In this sense, intentionally selecting powerful modes can contribute to an overall attempt to scaffold learning for the students.

Of course, care always needs to be taken when showing images of conflict and other traumatic aspects of the past. This is particularly the case when teaching students who have had some direct experience of conflict and violence.

Chapter summary

- History is a challenging and dynamic subject that can be lively and varied.
- Teachers need to be aware of the weight, energy and mode within and across their lessons to ensure that students do not become unnecessarily overwhelmed, learning opportunities are not missed, or that lessons become random and chaotic.
- Considering the weight of lessons involves reflecting on the intellectual and emotional demands of the content.
- Considering the energy of lessons involves reflecting on the drivers of cognitive activity and ensuring that this is not the sole responsibility of the teacher or the students.
- Considering the mode of lessons involves thinking about the medium(s) through which the past is explored in a topic and ensuring that these are genuine and valuable.

End of chapter questions

Questions for reflection and discussion	Questions to ask experienced teachers
1. Briefly summarise what you understand the terms weight, energy and mode to refer to in this context. 2. How might varying the weight, energy and mode be useful considerations for history teachers?	1. How do you avoid students getting overwhelmed when they are studying confronting topics or topics that are dense? 2. How do you vary activities in history classes but avoid classes becoming too chaotic or random? 3. How do you use audio-visual sources and objects in history?

Further reading

Resource	Why bother reading it?
Terry Epstein and Carla Peck (eds.), *Teaching and Learning Difficult Histories in International Contexts: A Critical Sociocultural Approach*, Routledge, 2019, pp. 82–94	This book offers a complex discussion of the challenges associated with teaching difficult histories. The chapters cover abstract themes and country-specific challenges.
Jade Pearce and Isaac Moore, *Desirable Difficulties in Action*, John Catt, 2024	Though not directly related to the teaching of history, many of the themes covered are generally useful for developing strategies to consider how we might calibrate the degree of challenge in teaching and learning.
Tsafrir Goldberg and Geerte Savenije, "Teaching Controversial Historical Issues", in Metzger, S., and Harris, L. (eds.) *The Wiley International Handbook of History Teaching and Learning*, John Wiley and Sons, 2018, pp. 503–26	Goldberg and Savenije offer considered and practical advice on teaching controversial historical issues that can add complexity to history lessons in secondary contexts.

CHAPTER 23

Revisit, consolidate and connect learning regularly

Revisiting and connecting material that you have been working through with your classes is crucial to helping students build their historical confidence. This will help the students develop a more secure and complex understanding or schema of the topics they have studied and will help the students synthesise knowledge and ideas and make meaning from what they have been learning. Regular revisits of the students' prior learning will also give you more opportunities for formative assessment that should help to ensure that your teaching is responsive to the students in your class.[82]

Establishing rhythm

Teachers have different preferences for how to revisit prior learning within their lessons, and there are many excellent approaches. Generally, I think it is helpful to use both smaller and larger revision tasks and make sure that these feature regularly across lessons.

Smaller tasks might include quicker activities such as teacher-directed questioning at the beginning of a lesson, brainstorms, and think-pair-share. Fortunately, many of these kinds of activities can be arranged without too much detailed teacher planning but they can be effective in helping students consolidate key aspects of their knowledge. I generally have a small suite of these preferred activities that I can call up at short notice and manage easily. This is particularly helpful if, for example, the students finish the main part of a lesson 5–10 minutes earlier than expected. In that situation, I can quickly select a simple activity that I know works well and use it to close off the lesson.

---

[82] Dylan Wiliam and Siobhan Leahy, *Embedding Formative Assessment: Practical Techniques for K–12 Classrooms*, Learning Sciences International, 2015.

Larger tasks might include quizzes, puzzles or more-difficult activities that take longer to complete. These tasks might involve more sustained effort on the students' behalf, such as a problem to solve that requires some reading, thinking and discussing or a piece of writing that draws upon previously learned material.

Over the duration of a topic, I try to establish a rhythm with these kinds of tasks. In simple terms, I generally use smaller revision tasks most regularly. In fact, I think some kind of revision and connection would take place in almost every lesson I teach so that students get used to this as a normal feature of the class. I then generally plan slightly larger tasks at more strategic junctures throughout a topic that bring together various features of a topic and require some synthesis and analysis.

Part of the aim of establishing this rhythm is so that students become more comfortable with the regular challenge of trying to recall key aspects of prior learning and use it to explain, analyse, argue and discuss. The hope is that the more they do this, the more natural it becomes and the more likely students are to make an effort as they see the benefits of the process.

Calibrating the level of challenge

It is important that revisiting prior learning is both challenging and rewarding for your students. If you consistently ask questions that are too difficult for anyone to answer during revision discussions, many students will quickly give up. At the same time, if the questions are too simple or repetitive, the challenge disappears and the process can easily become unrewarding. So, activities that require students to revise and consolidate prior learning should reveal and affirm what they know and are confident with but also stretch their memory and reveal areas of greater weakness so that they can correct, clarify and enrich their understanding. Pitching tasks that balance this can be difficult, and it takes time and practice to improve.

What should be revisited?

In secondary history, it can be difficult to decide on what students need to revisit and revise, because topics can include enormous amounts of information. When studying a unit on the Second World War, for example, would students need to remember which military units landed on which beaches on D-Day? Do they need to know the specific dates on which various agreements were signed? How many leading political figures' names should they remember? Given the immense complexity of the conflict, it would be impossible for them to remember everything, so what should be prioritised?

As with many other aspects of teaching secondary history, the answer to this question depends on many factors, including how old the students are and what kind of major assessment tasks they might be working towards. If there are external examinations, students may need to have a much more detailed knowledge of a wide range of themes and issues within the topic. In these cases, however, they should also be doing regular revision outside of class time too.

Systematic revision

When students are in senior years and are required to complete higher-stakes external examinations at the end of a course, it can be useful to require them to conduct systematic revision outside class time. This can be done in many ways, such as requiring them to produce revision notes and practise questions for each topic. These might be submitted for brief checking, comment and query as you work through key parts of the topic to ensure that students are making good progress and revising the material regularly.

In secondary history it is generally useful to begin planning revision around the most central concepts and ideas within a topic and then around those aspects of the topic that a class finds more complicated. For example, if you are teaching a topic on the Cold War, students must have a reasonable working knowledge of concepts such as communism, capitalism, domino theory, containment, and so on. In the early phases of this topic, prioritising these ideas for revision is important since the students are unlikely to make much real progress without a secure understanding of them. In this situation, if I create a revision quiz or discussion, I would prioritise questions around these concepts.

At different and appropriate points, students will also need to revisit more than substantive knowledge. If all you ever revisit in your history classes are the key dates, names, terms and facts related to a topic, students will miss opportunities to consolidate their understanding of key disciplinary and practical ideas that are also crucial to their success. In a topic covering the Middle Ages, for example, they might revise key terms and concepts, revise disciplinary ideas relating to change and continuity that you have foregrounded, and review key practical knowledge relating to how to make use of source material as they produce written explanations.

Consolidating and connecting knowledge

Although remembering key aspects of substantive, disciplinary and practical knowledge is crucial to gaining confidence in secondary history, students also need to do more than remember isolated factoids. Tom Sherrington makes this general point clear when he writes that:

> *Remembering takes many forms. When ... [activities are] more complex, less easy to define and control, messier, harder to give precise feedback on, they're probably going to deepen learning more than a daily quiz produced by the teacher can for the very reason that they are more complex, linking more ideas together. For some students, an overemphasis on quizzing processes may continually misfire because their experiential platform for the knowledge just isn't adequate or they can't apply the knowledge in new contexts due to lack of practice.*[83]

Furthermore, the most interesting aspects of history are often not the individual gobbets of information, but how these are placed together to create larger stories or make more complex connections and arguments. Once students' knowledge begins to grow more confident and secure, it is important that they have opportunities to make use of it in richer and more elaborate ways that capture the complex dimensions of historical work.

Consolidating knowledge

If you are studying a topic on the interwar dictatorships, for example, students will benefit from regular revision about the key facts of the regimes you explore: the names of key leaders, the years between which they ruled, key policy initiatives, the various uses of dictatorial power, and more. At some point, however, students' understanding will be enhanced by beginning to do more analytical work that might compare and contrast the regimes they have studied.

In his book *The Art and Science of Teaching* (2007), Rob Marzano offers some excellent ideas for consolidating and applying substantive knowledge in history. These are outlined and elaborated on in Table 23.1.

It is not difficult to imagine how similar strategies could be adapted when exploring empires, significant individuals, battles or conflicts, social movements, and many other common features of secondary history topics. These activities could be completed independently or collaboratively by

---

83 Tom Sherrington, "Schema-Building: A Blend of Experiences and Retrieval Modes Make for Deep Learning", 5 January 2020: https://teacherhead.com/2020/01/05/schema-building-a-blend-of-experiences-and-retrieval-modes-make-for-deep-learning/

getting students to work in pairs or small groups. Additionally, whole-class components could be added in which the teacher takes further opportunities by using follow-up questions to challenge students' knowledge and thinking (see below).

Not only should this kind of analytical work act as another revision opportunity as students think back over the material they have learned, but it also gives students an opportunity to begin thinking more analytically about the material, which is an essential part of doing history.

TABLE 23.1: Basic strategies for revising and consolidating substantive knowledge of interwar dictatorships using the suggestions of Rob Marzano[84]

	Description	Example
Comparing	Finding the similar and different characteristics of something.	List four similarities and four differences between the dictatorial approaches of Hitler and Stalin.
		Compare and contrast the use of propaganda in Nazi Germany under Hitler and in the USSR under Stalin in the 1930s.
Classifying	Placing specific examples into separate categories. Students could then explain or justify their choices.	Place the following regimes into the category of "authoritarian" or "totalitarian" based on the definition provided by Stephen Lee and justify your choices: Nazi Germany, the USSR (1930s), Fascist Italy, and Japan under Hideki Tojo.
		Place the following sources into categories using the following labels: propaganda, social history, political history, economic history.
Creating analogies	Finding parallels between different topics or examples.	The NKVD was to Stalin what the _____ was to Hitler.
		What event in Mussolini's rise to power might be considered the most similar to the Bolshevik seizure of power in October 1917? Justify your selection.

---

[84] Robert Marzano, *Art and Science of Teaching: A Comprehensive Framework for Effective Instruction*, Association of Supervision and Curriculum Development, 2007, pp. 71–77.

Connecting knowledge

In secondary history, students will also benefit from activities that require them to make broader connections between the material they are currently focusing on and material that they have previously learned.

Most obviously, if students are completing a topic that spans several weeks of class time and they are 75 percent of the way through, ensuring that key themes and ideas introduced in the earlier parts of a topic remain on the surface of their learning is important. This can be done by specifically requiring students to think and communicate about changes that they observe across the topic. For example, while exploring a topic on the First World War, studying the ways in which the conflict shaped the home fronts in Britain, France, Germany and Russia, the students might be asked to compare the state of those societies in 1914 and 1917. This might connect their study of the outbreak of war and initial reactions to how these attitudes shifted over time.

Connecting knowledge within a topic such as that outlined above is important, but it can also be useful to connect ideas across topics to help students consolidate their understanding of broader themes. For example, when studying conflicts in the 20th century, students might be specifically asked to think back over an earlier topic on the Industrial Revolution and consider how that earlier transformative event shaped the later conflict they are studying. This helps them make sense of the conflict in focus, but also reinforces and perhaps expands their knowledge of the legacies of the Industrial Revolution.

Class discussion and dialogue

Class discussion can be a powerful tool for consolidating and connecting knowledge in secondary history.[85] Well-structured and intentional discussions can help students deepen their understanding of the material they have explored and give them opportunities to experiment with their thinking as they express it in real time. Since history is a fundamentally contested discipline, debate and discussion are a natural feature of the subject and, for a teacher with confident subject knowledge, these can be lively and enjoyable ways of bringing learning to life. When done well, I have no doubt that this is one of the most enjoyable dimensions of history for many students.

---

[85] Carla van Boxtel and Jannet van Drie, "Engaging Students in Historical Reasoning: The Need for Dialogic History Education" in Carratero, M., Berger, S., and Grever, M. (eds.) *The Palgrave Handbook of Research in Historical Culture and Education*, Palgrave Macmillan, 2017, pp. 573–89.

These activities thrive in different contexts but most obviously once students have started to develop their knowledge about the topic or issue that they are exploring. Discussing what students already know about a topic can be useful to gain a sense of what they think before completing deep work, but I find that these activities are most productive once the students have made some progress with the topic. In these situations, you can begin to leverage their growing knowledge and help them apply it as they discuss and debate new questions that require them to rethink and reconsider what it is that they have learned. In particular, lengthy and robust class discussion can be important as students work towards large tasks in which they must create longer written responses that require analysis and judgment.[86] It can be helpful for many students to hear the ideas of others and refine their own thinking before they commit their ideas to paper or screen. This can also form a key part of the build-up scaffolding discussed in Chapter 17.

Personally, I try to make class discussions lively and interesting. I try to find challenging, interesting and perhaps even controversial questions to inject into the discussion that require students to make use of and apply their existing knowledge.

TABLE 23.2: Some basic tips for class discussion in secondary history

	Description	Example
Think-pair-share	This is an easy structure to manage, and it can be helpful to ensure higher participation rates (see below) within the class. The basic idea is to get students to respond to something individually (think), then discuss their response with another student or small group (pair), and then bring their ideas to a whole-class discussion.	Provide a one-sentence statement on the board in a class and require the students to quickly note down some initial reactions to it. Ask the students to join pairs or small groups and discuss their initial responses, making a note of similarities and differences. It is a good idea to circulate and listen in on discussions to get an idea of what ideas are emerging. Open a whole-class discussion. It can help to begin with some specific questions or even ask particular students to share their thoughts (this can be done in encouraging ways such as: "Jessica, as I was moving around, I heard what you were saying about X. I thought that was very interesting: could you please start by explaining…").

---

86 Richard Harris and Lorraine Foreman-Peck, "Learning to Teach History Writing: Discovering What Works", *Educational Action Research*, Vol. 9, No. 1, 2001, pp. 97–109.

	Description	Example
Public thinking activity	Sometimes, to ensure that all students begin to think about their response to a question or prompt, I require them to do something physical to identify their reaction. It is important that this is introduced as an activity capturing their provisional response and that there will be an opportunity to adjust their thinking as the discussion takes place. The aim here is to give all students something specific to think about and ensure that they all respond in some manner. It should provide the teacher with a quick and easy way to ask follow-up questions and get a more detailed discussion going.	Agree or disagree? Sometimes, it can be helpful to propose a claim and ask the students a concrete question such as: "Do you agree or disagree with this statement?" To get a quick insight into student responses, you might ask the whole class to stand up. Once standing, you then repeat the claim and ask all those who disagree to sit down. You can now select individual students and ask why they have sat down or remained standing and explore their ideas further (see the following row). To what extent do you agree? This might involve drawing a spectrum on the board with "agree" on one end and "disagree" on the other. You might then ask students to write their name on a Post-it note and place it along the line representing the degree to which they agree or disagree with a statement. You can then zero in on specific names and ask those students to elaborate on their thinking.
Probing questions	As students discuss the questions you pose (or they raise), asking follow-up questions that require them to elaborate, justify and extend their thinking can be powerful. Not only does this require them to revisit and connect more ideas, but it also gets them used to the process of arguing and communicating their points in a clear and concise manner.	Common follow-up questions or prompts useful to probing students' thinking in secondary history include: • Can you think of an example of what you have just said? • You have suggested X; what reasons do you have for making that claim? • If you are saying X, how would you respond to what Otis has just said about Y? • Tran has just made a very interesting point about X. Would anyone have a different perspective on that?

Keeping participation high

It is crucial in these kinds of activities that, as far as is reasonable, all students are required to participate. It is no good completing an in-class revision activity, for example, in which only four of the 27 students in the class are actively thinking while the rest daydream. In that scenario, it is entirely possible that 23 students are not thinking about the central issues that the activity targets and it is, therefore, entirely possible that they are learning very little.

To avoid this, it is important to try to find ways to ensure that all students are required to think and work during these tasks. Again, this can be done in simple ways that require minimum effort on the teacher's part, and some have already been hinted at in Table 23.2. These could include:

- Requiring all students to complete a quick and simple activity that can be visibly checked (such as a cloze passage). Here the teacher can circulate among the class, ask follow-up questions, keep students on task, and more.
- Getting the entire class to stand up before asking a true/false question and then requiring those who believe the statement to be false to sit down (meaning that those who remain standing are claiming that it is true). This can provide excellent opportunities for the teacher to ask follow-up question such as: "Jessica, you sat down. Can you please explain why you think this is false?"
- Quickly writing a couple of key terms on the board and asking all students to write down a brief definition of each and then discussing the responses.
- Posing a question and requiring the students to complete a quick "think-pair-share" activity.

Each of these simple activities requires all students to do something and, more importantly, think about the issues they have been studying. In each of these activities it is also reasonably easy to ensure that all students are participating and that each offers good opportunities for the teacher to ask follow-up questions and enrich the activity further if there is time and need.

Whatever the activity used to revise and consolidate students' understanding, it is important to ask: will this activity require all students to actively think about the material they have been studying?

Chapter summary

- Revisiting prior learning is a key aspect of effective teaching and learning.
- Activities that require students to revisit prior learning can be relatively quick and simple, or more sustained and elaborate.
- Planning to make these activities a regular aspect of your teaching will benefit the students, as they revise, consolidate and re-explore core ideas, and you as the teacher, who will be given regular opportunities to check the students' understanding, correct major errors, and plan for future activities.
- In secondary history, students need to revisit more than the substantive knowledge they have been learning. They should also revisit key disciplinary ideas and important aspects of practical knowledge they are required to work on, such as writing.

End of chapter questions

Questions for reflection and discussion	Questions to ask experienced teachers
1. Why is it important to revisit prior learning?	1. What kinds of material do you get students to revisit regularly in your classes?
2. What are some simple ways to get students to revisit prior learning? Can you think of some more complex ways to do this?	2. What kinds of activities do you use most regularly to get students to revisit prior learning?
3. Re-examine Table 23.1. Use the same ideas to come up with some activities for one or two other topics you will be required to teach in your jurisdiction.	3. How do you overcome student resistance to making an effort in these kinds of activities?
4. Why is it important to keep participation high in these activities? Can you think of other ways that this might be achieved?	

Further reading

Resource	Why bother reading it?
Tom Sherrington, "Schema-Building: A Blend of Experiences and Retrieval Modes Make for Deep Learning", 5 January 2020: https://teacherhead.com/2020/01/05/schema-building-a-blend-of-experiences-and-retrieval-modes-make-for-deep-learning/	This blog briefly outlines why it is important to avoid conflating good revision work with simply "quizzing" students on isolated information. One key aim of teaching is to help students develop large and more complex schemas of knowledge and understanding. Remembering basic factual information is unlikely to produce that, which means that revisiting learning must be more than quizzing and other basic checks of understanding.
Tom Sherrington, *Rosenshine's Principles in Action*, John Catt Educational Ltd, 2019	This short book includes a useful exposition of some key findings from the research of Barack Rosenshine. It includes helpful tips for revisiting prior learning with students.
Robert Marzano, *The Art and Science of Teaching: A Comprehensive Framework for Effective Instruction*, Association for Supervision and Curriculum Development, 2007 (Chapter 3: "What Will I Do to Help Students Practice and Deepen their Understanding of New Knowledge", pp. 58–85)	Marzano's book offers a range of practical ideas for approaching teaching. This chapter provides practical ideas that will help to deepen students' knowledge and understanding.
Jade Pearce and Isaac Moore, *Desirable Difficulties in Action*, John Catt, 2024	The "in action" series by publisher John Catt is a range of helpful books. Each is quite short and offers a snapshot of interesting and useful big ideas in education research. Though not directly related to the teaching of history, many of the themes covered are generally useful for developing strategies to revisit and consolidate understanding.

CHAPTER 24

Make stories and analogies a natural part of your teaching

Communicating about the past is deeply complex. History teachers need to develop a suite of strategies that help clarify, expand and challenge students' thinking in a manner that does justice to the past and that are pedagogically sensible. To do this we model, explain, connect, question, draw diagrams, create role-play scenarios, and more.

Fundamental to teaching history, however, are stories and analogies, which both carry profound opportunities to help students make sense of the past. They are, in addition, common ways of communicating about the past in everyday life and so they deserve our specific consideration.

Stories in secondary history

Humans thrive on narrative.[87] Not only do they help us organise large amounts of information, but stories about human ingenuity, mystery, trauma, determination, triumph and tragedy also have the power to arrest attention and stimulate our imagination. This is probably one of the reasons that history in the form of novels, films and shows thrives in the modern world.

Stories can also be powerful tools in secondary history since they can bind information together, make it memorable, and help students to arrange ideas into a more holistic view of the past.[88] The history teacher Emily Folorunsho captured this recently when she wrote:

> Stories make knowledge memorable, exciting and nourishing and our subject lends itself well to stories. When we use stories, we work with the

---

[87] Jag Bhalla, "It Is in Our Nature to Need Stories", *Scientific American*, 8 May 2013: https://www.scientificamerican.com/blog/guest-blog/it-is-in-our-nature-to-need-stories/
[88] Deb Hull, "Storytelling in History Teaching", *Agora*, Vol. 55, No. 2, 2020, pp. 3–5.

> *way the [human] brain most likes to organise information and create networks of connected ideas. Storytelling helps to humanise the past.*[89]

Stories might provide clarity for the direction of a topic or whole-year level and can also provide interesting and illuminating examples to consider when exploring different themes across time. They can also help to ensure that the perspectives we include in our lessons are appropriately varied and that we balance macro and micro scales to generate rich insights into the past.

Macro stories

Large-scale stories can be a useful way to frame entire topics and even whole-year levels in secondary history. They can provide a reference point for lessons and tasks and bind learning together over longer periods. Like the process of historical enquiry, narratives can help prevent secondary history from becoming atomised and unnecessarily confusing.

When I am teaching the formative period of Soviet history (1917–41), for example, I like to keep a broad story in view that helps students make sense of the various themes and developments. This story suggests that one of the most important overarching narratives of the period is a transition from party dictatorship under Vladimir Lenin during the years 1917–24 to a personal dictatorship under Joseph Stalin from 1928–41. To communicate this, I can use simple diagrams and a periodised timeline that give the students a cohesive sense of the topic. In addition, this overarching story allows me to link key themes and questions together to keep student attention focused on the most important issues of the topic.

Part of the challenge of developing these useable macro stories is that they require some degree of simplification, and this can be difficult. On the one hand, it is possible to develop an overarching story that is so oversimplified that it might become misleading or dilute the complexity of a topic to a damaging degree. On the other hand, if we try to capture all the complexities of a topic within an overarching narrative, it is likely to be too difficult, confusing and even counterproductive.

Like many other aspects of teaching secondary history, developing and using large narratives to help bring together key themes and questions of a topic requires practice. It also requires us to be transparent about the fact that these stories are open to contest and dispute (this will be discussed further below).

---

89 Emily Folorunsho, *Succeeding as a History Teacher*, Bloomsbury, 2024 p. 123.

Micro stories

Smaller-scale stories are equally important in secondary history. At a basic level, these might include anecdotes that we use to highlight a key issue in a topic or connect students to new material by making it relatable to something that they are more familiar with.

Historians regularly use well-chosen anecdotes to good effect in their work to capture our attention and also demonstrate how a broader theme might have been experienced "on the ground" during a specific period of time. We might, for example, discuss the experience of an individual suffragette campaigning to win the vote for women in the early 20th century. We might briefly consider the experience of an individual soldier to bring to light a key problem of warfare during a conflict that we are studying.

Secondary history also provides some opportunities to conduct periodic case studies that can enrich student understanding of broader abstract themes and larger scales of time.[90] These micro histories have been used powerfully by historians to raise important questions about controversial matters. For example, Christopher Browning conducted a study of a single German policing unit in his well-known *Ordinary Men: Reserve Police Battalion 101 and the Final Solution in Poland* (1992). This work engaged with important questions about the Holocaust using a case study, instead of beginning with a larger narrative or perspective. This scholarly method has given rise to what some have called "pedagogical micro history" as a tool for teaching aspects of history in different contexts.[91]

In secondary history we might make use of this method by selecting an individual, small group, single town or region as a case study that helps the students clarify, complicate and expand their understanding of key themes we explore across a broader topic. Well-selected case studies can also provide powerful opportunities to work closely with historical sources.

Analogies

Drawing helpful comparisons between what students might be more familiar with to illuminate and explain key aspects of the past can also be a powerful

---

90 Rachel Foster, "Compressing and Rendering: Using Biography to Teach Big Stories", *Teaching History*, Vol. 190, 2023, pp. 62–73.
91 See, for example, Graham Broad, *One in a Thousand: The Life and Death of Captain Eddy McKay, Royal Flying Corps*, University of Toronto Press, 2017, and Steven Bednarski, *A Poisoned Past: The Life and Times of Margarida de Portu, a Fourteenth-Century Accused Poisoner*, University of Toronto Press, 2014.

teaching tool in secondary history. In his recent book *History for Tomorrow* (2024), Thomas Krznaric wrote:

> *It is true that our ancestors were not entangled in digital networks or manipulating the human genome. But they were confronting many challenges that, in essence, mirror those of the present, from poverty and pandemics to warfare and water shortages. Analogies can also help to make connections across time: even a technology as apparently modern as artificial intelligence has its parallels in the past.*[92]

Helpful analogies can be varied depending of the issue and idea we are trying to communicate or clarify. Some simple examples are briefly outlined in Table 24.1.

TABLE 24.1: Common types of analogy for secondary history

History	Using stories and ideas from material that students have already studied can be a useful way to make connections between topics and leverage what students already know about the past to clarify new areas they are exploring. For example, when studying the Russian Revolution, you might use students' knowledge of the use of tsarist secret police to begin introducing the nature and role of the Soviet secret police.
Public	Contemporary public stories can be useful to clarify new ideas in secondary history. For example, in recent Australian politics, prime ministers have changed frequently, and bitter rivalries have played out in the media. These can be used to point out the ruthless nature of politics in many different historical contexts.
Personal	Personal stories can also be a way to illuminate aspects of the past. I vividly remember, for example, paying to shoot an AK-47 machine gun while travelling in Vietnam many years ago. I have often used that experience – the anxiety of squeezing the trigger and the furious noise exploding from the gun – when trying to explain why some people might have found firing weapons in war difficult or reading historical sources that describe the fear that warfare can easily induce.

Remaining selective and critical

It is crucial that we remain selective and critical in our approach to using stories and analogies in secondary history. The aim is not to overwhelm students with too many stories or comparisons such that these become the

---

92 Thomas Krznaric, *History for Tomorrow: Inspiration from the Past for the Future of Humanity*, WH Allen, 2024, p. 8.

main aspects of a topic that students most remember. The aim is always to ensure that these assist students' understanding of key historical ideas and make it easier for them to make sense of new information or integrate new knowledge.

To do this, we need to be careful in choosing the stories and analogies we make use of. It can be tempting, for example, to tell ripping tales or focus on gory details, since these often generate strong reactions from students. Although these may be important to a topic and perfectly justifiable, it is also easy for them to overshadow other crucial ideas in a topic without students learning or remembering much beyond the story itself.

In addition, we need to be open with students about the fact that the stories we tell and the analogies we use are ultimately open to question and contest. The passage by Thomas Krznaric quoted above goes on to add:

> ... *[when considering analogies] it is key to highlight differences [between present and past] as much as similarities, and be wary of making simplistic or misplaced comparisons: every dictator is not another Adolf Hitler, every war is not another Vietnam, every economic crisis is not another Wall Street Crash.*[93]

Not only can we be directly honest about this open-endedness, but we can also use the stories and analogies as specific activities in class. We might, for example, closely examine an analogy and question the degree to which it applies. We might also ask the students to provide an alternative analogy or story that captures a topic, theme or idea more accurately.

Finding stories and analogies

The ability to confidently and clearly use stories and analogies in secondary history is intimately linked with subject expertise. Teachers with more confident subject knowledge and experience are more likely to be able to find and deploy stories and analogies in ways that are powerful.

As you begin your history teaching career, it is important to actively look for stories and analogies that can be used in your classes. As you work on developing your subject expertise (see Chapter 2), remain observant as you read or listen to historians talk about their work.

More practically, useful stories and analogies can be gleaned from:

- Reading historical works

---

[93] Thomas Krznaric, *History for Tomorrow: Inspiration from the Past for the Future of Humanity*, WH Allen, 2024, p. 8.

- Listening to podcasts in which hosts or guests use stories, anecdotes and analogies to communicate about the past
- Examining primary sources that might include vivid stories about a topic that you teach
- Visiting sites and museums that might provide examples of objects or spaces that can help illuminate aspects of the past.

Most importantly, you will need to begin experimenting with using narratives, anecdotes and analogies in your teaching. Try introducing a lesson with a story or include a brief anecdote or analogy when explaining a concept to a student who has asked an important question. The more you use these devices, the more comfortable you will become in naturally incorporating them into your teaching.

Chapter summary

- Narrative is a crucial dimension of history.
- Macro stories can be used to bring coherence to whole topics and year levels.
- Micro stories can be used to illuminate key themes and explore history from unique perspectives.
- Analogies can be a powerful tool to help students make sense of new material and relate aspects of history to more familiar knowledge they already possess.
- Stories and analogies should be used intentionally and in an open-ended manner.

End of chapter questions

Questions for reflection and discussion	Questions to ask experienced teachers
1. What kinds of historical stories do you most enjoy?	1. What kinds of stories do you use most in your teaching?
2. Did any of your teachers at school or university use stories or analogies effectively? What did they do that was helpful?	2. How do you find new stories and analogies to use in your teaching?
3. In what ways are stories and analogies most helpful in secondary history?	
4. What caution needs to be taken with the use of stories and analogies?	

Further reading

Resource	Why bother reading it?
Deb Hull, "Storytelling in History Teaching", *Agora*, Vol. 55, No. 2, 2020, pp. 3–5	This article develops some important arguments about the role and importance of story in secondary history.
Jonathan Grande, "#11 This Week, in History… I'm Remembering to Make My Teaching Memorable", 19 February 2023: https://curricularpasts.wordpress.com/2023/02/19/11-this-week-in-history-im-remembering-to-make-my-teaching-memorable/	One of Grande's arguments in this blog post is that stories can help to clarify important ideas in history, but also make them more memorable. He offers some important pointers for using stories in history and shares a range of useful examples.

CHAPTER 25

Save time with some templates that you can adapt

The term "template" can raise hairs on the backs of some teachers' necks, and for good reason. Some schools or jurisdictions go overboard in prescribing particular templates and resources that teachers *must* use in their units of work, in the mistaken view that this generic imposition will somehow magically secure higher standards and save teachers' time. Centrally mandated resources and materials can be useful, but their benefits are often exaggerated given the complexities of school life.

In this particular context, I am using the term "template" to refer to a helpful framework or activity that *you* have created or selected that you reuse and adapt in different contexts. It does not refer to a mandatory or rigid idea that should limit what you do. In other words, a template in this context is a useful activity or general structure for a lesson that you find works and that can be repeated across multiple topics and age-groups without too much planning involved. Importantly, because you have selected it, the template remains in your control and can be adapted or even discarded as you see fit.

Basic lesson introduction templates

I would argue that there is absolutely no sense as a beginning or early-career history teacher trying to dream up a uniquely creative introduction to every single lesson you teach. That is likely to be a colossal waste of time and energy. Instead, it might be worth trying to think of four or five effective introductions that work for you that can be repeated across topics and year groups as a foundation from which you can then build.

Here are some simple examples I still rely on and improvise with regularly, all of which are probably as old as modern education in some form or another:

- **Teacher summary and orientation:** This is probably the simplest of all and involves the teacher briefly but clearly reminding students of essential themes and ideas that they have been learning and what the direction for the current lesson will be. This could be completed in under a minute or be expanded with some spontaneous questioning of the students regarding what they previously learned. Again, this involves almost no preparation on the teacher's part provided you are confident in quickly generating a succinct summary of previous learning, something that all teachers should aim to improve at quickly.

- **Direct questioning and discussion:** Sometimes, once the class has entered the room and is seated, I will simply begin asking specific students questions related to the content we have been learning. These could be targeted towards eliciting essential knowledge, checking on a concept or procedure, or even discussing a contemporary event to make links to important ideas in the lesson or sequence. As the students begin to settle into the lesson, this might turn into a more free-flowing discussion that I then use to pivot to the day's work. Sometimes I even try to make it fun and interesting, so long as it does not unsettle the class or distract from the learning goals.

- **Simple task on the board to get started:** In some contexts, it is now popular to call this a "do now" activity, which is probably a catchier and more marketable label for what is actually a very old and simple idea. This involves greeting a class at the door and asking them to enter and begin working on a short activity. This should be simple, succinctly expressed, and easy to monitor and follow up. For example: "Turn to a new page in your book (or open a new document) and brainstorm everything you can remember from this topic so far." I might alter the "everything you can remember from the topic" by focusing, for example, on a main theme or concept from the topic. Ideally this should require minimal clarification and, if done correctly, will mean that every student has begun to work cognitively and can be called upon to contribute an idea from their brainstorming once the main part of the lesson begins. This requires almost no preparation on your part as the teacher.

- **Think-pair-share:** Once I am more confident that I have control of my class and they know the routines I tend to work with, I might begin a lesson with some mini-group work. For example, I might have a primary source photograph projected on the board in the room and ask the students to discuss in pairs what they notice in the image. They will then be called upon to share their ideas and I will use these collective contributions to pivot to the focus of today's lesson.

I can use a version of each of these introductions with almost any age-group in any topic that I am working through and, best of all, they require little planning and effort. They are lesson introduction templates that I employ regularly and continue to experiment with.

At this point, it is important to note that there are also times when I do not use a dedicated "starter activity" at the beginning of a lesson. In Chapter 12 we discussed the importance of breaking topics into meaningful parts and moving away from the "individual lesson view" of planning. For my teaching, I think mostly in terms of whole topics and sequences of lessons rather than individual lessons. This means that two or three lessons can run fairly seamlessly into each other. In such cases, I sometimes begin those lessons with a quick check-in with the students and let them continue working on whatever their task is. This is particularly the case with older students, classes I have developed an efficient working relationship with, and when I see a class regularly throughout the week or on consecutive days.

Basic lesson structure templates

More broadly, a second example of how I might use templates in my planning is in overall lesson structure. Again, it would make no sense to try to heroically stay up to 3am every morning planning highly creative lessons for every single class you teach. It would be wonderful if every lesson left students buzzing with excitement, thanking you profusely for your efforts each time they walked out the door, but that is a dream that few, if any, teachers will experience in their career. Of course, that does not mean you should be discouraged from trying to infuse your lessons with enthusiasm and creativity, but it is also possible for this to become an unnecessary burden.

Instead of burning out trying to be the creative hero, I tend to think that it is more reasonable to aim to teach quality lessons consistently and then become more creative over time as your confidence grows. To develop consistency, it would make sense to begin by thinking about some strong and dependable lesson structures that can be adapted for multiple topics and multiple ages. To do this, consider lesson templates that, when combined into a sequence, address each aspect of the "content, complexity, communication" approach introduced in Chapter 16.

Some concrete examples that are likely to be useful in most topics might include:

- **The documentary lesson (a content-focused lesson):** When I am planning new units of work, I almost always look for an overview documentary or video that I can use in the first week or two that provides a good overview of the chronology, themes and issues central to the topic. If I have time, I prefer to write out guided questions for these videos and require the students to write notes in response to these questions as the film plays. In early parts of the film, I will pause and check that students have been gathering information for the questions to model the notetaking I am expecting and check that they have understood key ideas. I will then roam the room and make sure students are taking useful notes as the documentary plays. I can do this in some form for almost every topic I teach in secondary history.

- **The textbook lesson (a content-focused lesson):** Though you may not plan to use a textbook for every lesson with your classes, these can be extremely useful when employed intentionally. Decent textbooks should include a variety of material that can be adapted with your classes, including narrative text, source material, guided questions, and more. With some structure around it and active involvement by the teacher, two or three pages of a textbook can easily provide the foundation for a strong lesson or two. For example, you might start with an introductory activity such as some spontaneous questioning of the class to connect the lesson to prior learning. Then you might read a narrative section of the textbook with the class pausing to discuss and clarify important points or make connections with material already learned. You might then get the students to individually respond to some guided questions, roam the room to check in on students' progress and the quality of their work, and then use these responses as the basis for some whole-class discussion and feedback. If you know a topic reasonably well, such a lesson would require almost no detailed preparation if your overall planning for the topic is in order. Additionally, a similarly structured lesson could easily move into exploring the complexity of a topic if there are quality sources or historians' interpretations provided in the section of the book you are working with.

- **The sources lesson (a complexity-focused lesson):** In Chapter 16 we explored the flexible "content, complexity, communication" approach to sequences of lessons. Often when I try to explore the complexity within a sequence, it involves working with carefully selected source material that deepens students' substantive knowledge of what we are studying and helps them work with disciplinary concepts such as evidence or perspectives. It can take some time to find these sources, but the structure of these lessons tends to follow a fairly repeatable rhythm for me. We start the lesson with some review of the content, I introduce the sources we will explore by perhaps working through one with them together, and then I get the students to work independently or in groups (depending on how many sources there are and what I am aiming to achieve). Again, I use that basic structure in most year groups and in almost any topic in which I am exploring sources. Crucially, it remains flexible in that I might add other processes or activities or change the order.

- **The writing lesson (a communication-focused lesson):** Though there is often a lot of content to get through in history, it is important that you plan class time for some written work. This way you can model the form, style and quality of the writing, reiterate the requirements of a task, check student understanding, and allow the students to ask questions. Keeping in mind that I try to remain agile, for me these lessons tend to have common components: introduce or remind students of the requirements of the task, model and discuss the format and expectations, then allow students time to write their responses while I roam and assist. Sometimes, I might add other aspects, depending on the length of the writing. For example, I might examine additional sample pieces of similar work before they begin as an extended component of the modelling. Or, I might plan that the students will finish with enough time to complete some peer feedback on the finished product.

These basic examples are not meant to impress anyone for their ingenuity. They are lesson templates that I think teachers have been using for many years. But strong and effective teaching does not need to be mind-blowingly creative every day. In addition, I have found that developing a suite of lesson templates that I can confidently rely on means that I am then more likely to have additional time and energy to develop some other creative resources, assessments or lesson sequences. Sometimes, choosing to be less creative in one area of teaching allows you to be more creative in another.

Other basic templates

These bread-and-butter examples are also designed to prompt you to consider other templates that you might use to help build an initial catalogue of flexible, effective and workable activities and lessons. Some other templates that I tend to keep in my kit include (and these may be individual lessons or sequences of lessons):

- **A library lesson** – learning to use academic databases for research (sometimes with the assistance of a teacher-librarian)
- **A computer lesson** – student collaboration on work using a cloud-based platform

- **A discussion or debate lesson** – structured debate interrogating a key idea or question in depth often towards the end of a major section of a topic
- **An essay-planning lesson** – developing a structured response to a complex question with a scaffold but not a full written response
- **A popular film study lesson** – assessing an extract of a film for its historical value
- **A student-led lesson** – in which the students develop questions through which to explore a topic in more depth or from new perspectives (this could easily then lead into time researching in a library or on devices)
- **A museum exhibition lesson** – assessing an exhibition (or part of an exhibition) for its historical value
- **An artificial intelligence lesson** – prompting, assessing and reviewing historical ideas presented by an artificial intelligence platform to assist in the generation of research and investigation
- **A guest-speaker lesson** – working with the perspective of a guest-speaker (live or virtual) to add depth and personal immediacy to a topic.

This list could be extended and be far more creative than this. In fact, it is likely that as you grow in experience and confidence as a teacher, the list of "templates" that you can quickly and effortlessly draw on and adapt will grow and become more impressive. But it would be unwise to expect that this will be the case too quickly.

Chapter summary

- Developing flexible templates of your own can be a way to cut down on planning time while ensuring that your teaching remains high quality.
- Templates that are rigid or imposed can be counter-productive, but those that you are familiar with and find useful can free up time to be creative in other areas of your teaching.

End of chapter questions

Questions for reflection and discussion	Questions to ask experienced teachers
1. Examine the list of templates outlined in this chapter. Have you used any of these or seen them work well in action? What made them effective? 2. Why is it important to balance creativity and practicality in teaching?	1. Do you have any go-to lesson structures that you use when you have not had time to do detailed planning for a class?

Further reading

Resource	Why bother reading it?
Robert Marzano, *The Art and Science of Teaching: A Comprehensive Framework for Effective Instruction*, Association for Supervision and Curriculum Development, 2007 (Chapter 10: "What Will I Do to Develop Effective Lessons Organized into a Cohesive Unit", pp. 174–90)	Marzano's book offers a range of practical ideas for approaching teaching. This chapter sets out helpful tips to ensure that the "infrastructure" planned for approaching topics and lessons is logical and helpful. Although the ideas are not history-specific, many of the principles provide helpful direction for planning teaching and learning in history classes.

CHAPTER 26

Make intentional use of feedback

Feedback is a crucial part of teaching and learning. If we are to help students make progress and continue to develop their historical confidence and agility, then providing them with clear ideas about how they might make incremental steps forward is essential.

And yet, there is no guarantee that the feedback teachers provide is always helpful.[94] Writing detailed comments on student essays might seem intuitive or mimic what we have seen other teachers doing, but it is by no means certain that the time spent doing this is always the best way to help students improve. Planning to include feedback into the regular processes of teaching and learning is certainly important, but it needs to be thought about reflectively and intentionally if it is to be successful.

Feedback modes

There are multiple modes of feedback available to secondary history teachers that can all be leveraged to assist student progress. These can be used in combination over time to provide clear directions to students and to ensure that teachers' workloads do not balloon unnecessarily.

Most obviously, teachers can provide reasonably continuous feedback in the lesson-to-lesson work with classes. This can include whole-class feedback during activities, individualised comments as teachers move around a class and monitor work, and corrections to verbalised responses during class discussions.

When it comes to larger tasks, other feedback modes can also be used to help support students. Some of these are outlined in Table 26.1.

---

[94] Avraham Kluger and Angelo DeNisi, "The Effects of Feedback Interventions on Performance: A Historical Review, a Meta-Analysis, and a Preliminary Feedback Intervention Theory", *Psychological Bulletin*, Vol. 199, No. 2, 1996, pp. 254–84.

TABLE 26.1: Some different forms of more-formal feedback often used in combination in secondary history

Written comments	Providing students with individualised written comments on their work can be a useful way to directly encourage them and to offer itemised suggestions for their continued improvement. It can also help to keep a record of your direct feedback to them.
Rubrics	These provide descriptions of common mistakes/problems with a particular task and general suggestions for student improvement. These can be helpful for tasks in secondary history such as essays where mistakes can be common and do not always need highly specified or individualised comments.
Verbal: individual	Speaking directly with students in a supportive manner can also provide additional insights into their work. You might use this to clarify or extend written comments.
Verbal: whole class	Discussing tasks with an entire class before providing more individualised feedback can assist in reinforcing important ideas about key procedures and help the students make additional sense of other forms of feedback they might receive.
Peer	In the context of a safe and supportive classroom culture, requiring students to work together to provide feedback on each other's work can be a powerful way for students to be directly involved in the process of improving.
Self-reflective	Requiring students to assess their own work – perhaps with a delay between completion and analysis – can be a useful way of ensuring that students specifically examine their work and generate clearer plans for their own path towards improvement.

These modes of feedback can often be combined to ensure that teacher workloads remain more sustainable, students receive different perspectives on their work, and students are directly and actively involved in the process of giving and receiving feedback. Once essays have been submitted, for example, a teacher might take these home for individualised marking and feedback. Before providing the students with their feedback, the teacher might then require the students to re-read their work a week or two later and collate their own analysis by pointing out strengths, weaknesses and strategies for improvement based on a general rubric provided by the teacher. Finally, the teacher might provide each student with their feedback and discuss the similarities and differences between it and the students' own perceptions to create a shared understanding about what the student might address to make incremental progress in the area of essay writing. In this case, the student has received multiple forms of feedback and also been required to be active in the process.

Prioritising suggestions for improvement

In secondary history, students can often submit work for feedback that requires a range of different refinements. In a persuasive essay, for example, a student's overall argument may be inconsistent, their writing may have slipped away from analysis and argument towards summarising or recounting a narrative, they may have inconsistently used sources and/or evidence, and they may have included a range of factual and spelling errors across the piece.

In situations such as this, it is important to provide a constructive frame for your feedback by ensuring that the student's real achievements are identified and affirmed. The fact that the student submitted a complete and roughly structured essay might, for example, be a major improvement on their previous efforts. It can also be important that we do not barrage the student with an overwhelming list of every adjustment or correction that they would need to make to their work.

In these scenarios, I often try to prioritise my feedback to students to ensure that they concentrate on improving the most important dimensions of their work first. In an essay, for example, if a student does not sustain a clear and consistent line of argument, I would prioritise this in my feedback, since it is critical to all of the essays they will ever write in the subject. If they have made some minor factual errors in the piece, I would also point these out but, if I am providing written comments, I would spend more time commenting on the argumentative structure than on itemising every factual mistake in written form. If the student can improve the argumentative structure of their essays, their return on investment of effort will be more significant in the longer term than if they fix every minor error in their writing but pay no attention to the overall structure of the writing.

To be clear, I am not suggesting here that if students make factual or spelling errors, these should be ignored. Instead, I might provide a major comment about the argumentative structure in my written feedback as a key priority for improvement and then point out the most important factual errors verbally or with brief in-text annotations. If a student cannot create and sustain an argument in a history essay, it would be no good spending copious amounts of time explaining all the minor factual errors, since this would leave the overarching problem with their work untouched.

I often refer to this idea of prioritising feedback as "working from the inside out", referring to diagram 26.1.

DIAGRAM 26.1: Working from the inside out in providing feedback on essay-writing: what will improve the students' work most in the mid-to-longer term?

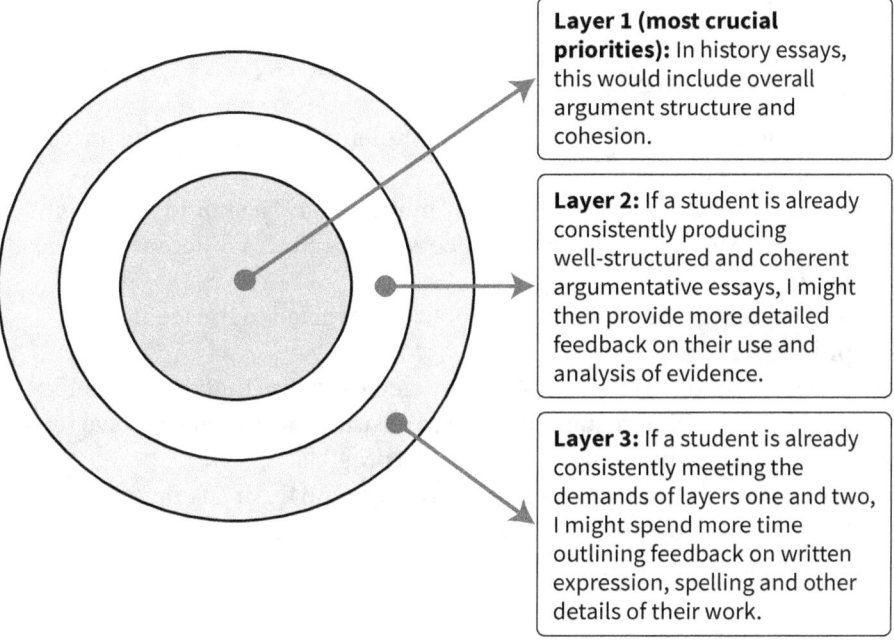

Layer 1 (most crucial priorities): In history essays, this would include overall argument structure and cohesion.

Layer 2: If a student is already consistently producing well-structured and coherent argumentative essays, I might then provide more detailed feedback on their use and analysis of evidence.

Layer 3: If a student is already consistently meeting the demands of layers one and two, I might spend more time outlining feedback on written expression, spelling and other details of their work.

Student involvement in the feedback process

It is crucial that students are actively involved in the feedback process. If you merely write comments and assume that they have been read, you are likely to be disappointed. Students study many subjects and are busy people too; even the most dedicated can forget key suggestions or mistake the key messaging in the feedback they receive. Other students simply may not read written comments carefully without a requirement to do so.

It is, therefore, important that students' active involvement becomes a natural part of the feedback process. Over time, they should come to expect that they will be required to think specifically about their work and contribute to plans that will help them improve in incremental ways. This can be a challenge, since openly discussing the strengths and weaknesses of one's own performance can be difficult for even the most confident people.

Table 26.1 has already outlined some specific ways in which students might be required to engage in the feedback process. In addition, some specific examples of how they could be involved have been outlined. Part of the overall aim of including students in the feedback process is to ensure that they remain cognitively active, but also to help build, as far as possible, a culture of shared progress and achievement.

Chapter summary

- Feedback is a crucial part of helping students improve their historical agility and confidence.
- Feedback is not synonymous with "marking", and it should be thought of as both a formal and informal process that occurs in different ways over time.
- It is important for students to be actively involved in the feedback process.
- Different modes of feedback can be used to ensure that the teacher's workload remains sustainable and to ensure that students receive high-quality commentary on their work and progress.
- Sometimes it can be important to prioritise the feedback provided to students so that they are not overwhelmed by exhausting lists of actionable comments.

End of chapter questions

Questions for reflection and discussion	Questions to ask experienced teachers
1. What kinds of feedback did you find most/least helpful at school or university? 2. What kinds of feedback have you seen work well in schools so far? 3. Why is it important to ensure that students are actively involved in the feedback process?	1. What kinds of feedback do you mostly use in secondary history? 2. How do you ensure that students are actively involved in the process of giving and receiving feedback?

Further reading

Resource	Why bother reading it?
Rachel Ball and Kyle Graham, "Giving Meaningful Feedback", in Fairlamb, A., and Ball, R. (eds.) *What Is History Teaching Now? A Practical Handbook for All History Teachers and Educators*, John Catt, 2023, pp. 301–10	In their chapter on feedback in secondary history, Rachel Ball and Kyle Graham offer discussion of four different strategies for feedback commonly used by history teachers (live feedback, spotlight examples, whole-class feedback and exam feedback).
Carl Hendrick, "Four Quarters Marking: A Workload Solution" (interview with Dylan Wiliam): https://carlhendrick.com/2017/09/02/four-quarters-marking-a-workload-solution/	This short blog summarises an interview with Dylan Wiliam about feedback in schools. It briefly captures Wiliam's suggestion about using different kinds of feedback to ensure that teachers' workload is more sustainable and to ensure that students are active participants in the process. Although I do not personally use the "four quarters" suggestions specifically, it is another useful tool that can be adapted in secondary history.

Epilogue

I consider the ideas in this book as foundational to my current view of history teaching, not horizons.

The chapters here do, I hope, bring together some important ideas relating to the teaching of secondary history that give the role of a beginning history teacher some intellectual and practical cohesion. Although they cannot be exhaustive, they can, I think, be intelligently adapted for many contexts.

In his book *The Mystery of Things* (2004), the philosopher Anthony Grayling argued that:

> *Knowledge is a great treasure, but there is one thing higher than knowledge, and that is understanding. Mere information by itself is worth little, unless it is arranged in ways that make sense to its possessors, and enables them to act effectively and live well. To make sense of information – to understand it – one has to put it into fruitful relationship with other information, and grasp the meaning of that relationship, which implies finding patterns, learning lessons, drawing inferences, and as a result seeing the whole. This task – achieving understanding – is par excellence the task of philosophy... There are many resources people can use to attain understanding, but three are of special value to philosophy, because they supply the best materials for reflection. They are science, history and the arts. These enterprises are lenses that bring into focus the three connected things we most wish to grasp: the world of nature, the nature of humanity, and the value in both.*[95]

I have had this quote on my wall in one form or another for about 15 years. It is not only a source of inspiration, because I think Grayling makes a powerful argument for the importance of history, but also a deep challenge, since how we might put knowledge into fruitful relationship with other knowledge and what it might mean to explore "the nature of humanity" is intensely complex.

This is one of the reasons that I think it is crucial for history teachers to keep wide eyes on the discipline of history and wide eyes on the profession of

---

95 Anthony Grayling, *The Mystery of Things*, Phoenix, 2004, p. 1.

teaching more generally. No matter how confident one becomes as a teacher, there is always the possibility that new inflections and perhaps even brave new ideas are just out of sight. There may be, to use Grayling's comment, new ways of putting old knowledge into relationship with new ideas.

E. H. Carr famously tried to capture this by suggesting that history is an "unending dialogue between the present and the past".[96] Not only do our knowledge of the past and ways of exploring it evolve, but so do the political, economic and social conditions of the present.[97]

There is currently complex and challenging work being done, for example, by historians and teachers on issues relating to education and history in the Anthropocene.[98] As the father of a four-year-old, I am excited by the possibilities this work holds out and believe that it will help to refine the way history education is conceptualised and practised.

Historians and teachers are also working on ways in which our knowledge of deep time adds to and challenges our view of the past and the discipline of history. In Australian history this has become prominent in the last two decades, and there has been much professional discussion around how the insights of deep time might influence history education.[99]

There is exciting work too that challenges the ways in which we perceive the discipline of history and the role of historians in society. In *Time's Monster* (2020) Priya Satia has called specific attention to the ways in which historians were entangled in empire, and Anna Clark has asked difficult questions about the boundaries we place on history in *Making Australian History* (2022). Other scholars continue to challenge the way in which the subject has been framed in schools and the kinds of content and epistemologies that are often privileged.[100]

This debate is, in my view, all healthy and natural. Despite some confident pronouncements that "scientific history" could banish ignorance and lead humanity to a finally true knowledge of the past, there has probably never

---

96 Edward Hallett Carr, *What Is History? (2nd Ed.)*, Penguin Books, 1987, p. 30.
97 A good follow-up to E. H Carr's 1961 classic is Suzannah Lipscomb and Helen Carr (eds.), *What Is History Now? How the Past and Present Speak to Each Other*, Weidenfeld and Nicolson, 2022.
98 See Heather McGregor, Jackson Pind and Sarah Karn, "A 'Wicked Problem': Rethinking History Education in the Anthropocene", *Rethinking History*, Vol. 25, No. 4, 2021, pp. 483-507, Kate Hawkey, *History and the Climate Crisis: Environmental History in the Classroom*, UCL Press, 2023, and Social Studies & History Education in the Anthropocene Network: https://sshean.ca/project/
99 See Volume 56 (Issue 1) of *Teaching History*, published by the History Teachers' Association of New South Wales in 2022, which was dedicated to the theme of deep history.
100 Matilda Keynes, "History Education for Transitional Justice? Challenges, Limitations and Possibilities for Settler Colonial Australia", *International Journal of Transitional Justice*, Vol. 13, No. 1, 2019, pp. 113-33.

been a time when the discipline of history has stood still or when at least some scholars have not challenged dominant forms of the subject.[101] In fact, part of the argument of this book is that, to understand history, students need to become comfortable with a degree of debate and open-endedness that lies at the subject's heart. If we cannot rest confidently in this as teachers when it comes to our subject, it seems difficult to imagine how students might become mature in their attitudes and reactions to history.

All of this is to reiterate a fundamental theme of this book: to encourage history teachers to think carefully about their work. As noted in the introduction, Bob Bain has argued that one of the challenges for secondary history teachers is that they must remain "bifocal by pursuing both *historical* [disciplinary] and *instructional* [pedagogical] lines of thinking".[102] Since we would expect both of these dimensions of our work to evolve, we must be prepared to balance whatever convictions we develop with an open-mindedness that these can, and probably inevitably will, change in some areas.

In this quest, I have benefited enormously from the community of history teachers now increasingly connected around the world. Despite a shared commitment to the subject and its importance in schools, this community includes a wide variety of perspectives and approaches, and I have no doubt that many would disagree with aspects of what I have written here – I have tried to be transparent about some of these differences in the footnotes and suggestions for further reading throughout the book.

Becoming a confident history teacher is ultimately a long game, but it is, fortunately, not a solitary or static one. We all have to develop our own ways of approaching the many challenges of teaching secondary history, but we can benefit enormously from the collective wisdom we have easier access to in the 21st century. It is, therefore, important to remain connected to local, national and global networks of history teachers who can provide inspiration, guidance, support and challenge in what is ultimately a demanding yet rewarding endeavour.

My basic hope in writing this book was to make a small and constructive contribution to this growing network of people and ideas. I hope that, in some ways at least, it inspires you, challenges you, and ultimately helps you take some positive steps towards a strong foundation for a rewarding career.

---

101 Daniel Woolf, *A Global History of History*, Cambridge University Press, 2011.
102 Robert Bain, "'They Thought the World Was Flat?' Applying the Principles of How People Learn in Teaching High School History", in Donovan, S., and Bransford, J. (eds.) *How Students Learn: History in the Classroom*, National Academies Press, 2005, p. 182.

www.ingramcontent.com/pod-product-compliance
Lightning Source LLC
Chambersburg PA
CBHW070405120526
44590CB00014B/1273